The Star Qualities

The Star Qualities

*How to sparkle with confidence
in all aspects of your life*

Caroline Goyder

SIDGWICK & JACKSON

First published 2009 by Sidgwick & Jackson
an imprint of Pan Macmillan Ltd
Pan Macmillan, 20 New Wharf Road, London N1 9RR
Basingstoke and Oxford
Associated companies throughout the world
www.panmacmillan.com

ISBN 978-0-283-07104-1 (HB)
ISBN 978-0-283-07102-7 (TPB)

1 3 5 7 9 8 6 4 2

A CIP catalogue record for this book is available
from the British Library.

Printed and bound in the UK by
CPI Mackays, Chatham ME5 8TD

Visit **www.panmacmillan.com** to read more about all our books
and to buy them. You will also find features, author interviews and
news of any author events, and you can sign up for e-newsletters
so that you're always first to hear about our new releases.

To the students and staff of
Central School of Speech and Drama

Contents

INTRODUCTION

The Star Qualities

Shakespeare famously wrote that all the world's a stage. He was right. The moment you step out of your door, you step into the theatre of life. You're *on*. You can stutter and apologize for your presence, or you can step forward with the confidence and poise to star in your life.

It takes courage and skill to stand out from the crowd. Actors can help you shine, because they have learned the art of being poised in public. They know how to seem at ease in themselves when the lights go up. Actors may seem sublimely confident, but underneath the cool surface they get as terrified as the rest of us. You don't *see* it, because the trained actor is equipped with a toolkit which gives them a tremendous advantage in tricky moments. I want to share that toolkit with you, to help you face real life challenges with calm and charisma.

I trained as an actor and now train actors at London's Central School of Speech and Drama. I also work with a wide range of individuals to teach them acting techniques to apply in their everyday lives. I've seen people conquer their fears, let go of their inhibitions and achieve their dreams. You can too.

The actors you will meet in these pages are not only masters of their craft, but also down to earth enough to know how to apply their professional skills to real-life challenges. Sarah Jessica Parker, Kate Winslet, Helen Mirren, Frances McDormand, Ewan McGregor and Gael Garcia Bernal are just a few of the leading actors of our time who have generously joined with me to share their experiences so that you can shine in the theatre of life.

These actors know at first hand how scary performance can be, and have revealed the techniques which allow them to stand in front of others and to be, *or to seem* calm and confident. This knowledge from the acting world, combined with their personal secrets and tips, will help you handle your parties, presentations, interviews and dates – with polish and panache. You'll get great jobs, sparkle at parties, and dazzle the gorgeous stranger!

Above all, I want my book to give you the confidence to get past your self-doubt so that you can really shine in your life. That's what I call real star quality.

The world is your stage. Relax. Breathe. Smile. You're *on*!

CHAPTER 1

Stand Out from the Crowd

*We must overcome the notion that we must be
ordinary . . . it robs you of the chance to be
extraordinary and leads you to the mediocre.*

UTA HAGEN

*Other people have a lot of plans for you –
but passion and authenticity will find you freedom
and power. It takes courage to do what you want.*

SUSAN SARANDON

How to Find Your Confidence and Your Charisma

Oscar Wilde lamented that there was so little star quality around, writing that, 'Most people are other people . . . their lives a mimicry, their passions a quotation.'

If you want to be outstanding, you must find the courage to stand out. Star quality is about having the mettle to follow your own path. Barack Obama was told at Harvard that his poor skills as an orator would prevent him from becoming a great politician. He was advised to stick to law lecturing. Barack Obama listened politely and then made up his own mind.

It's not easy to stand out – it can feel scary. The reason for this fear makes sense when you remember that on your own in a primitive society you didn't stand a chance. This fear of isolation has left a legacy in modern times. Psychologists call it 'group-think': people become so seduced by the safety of the group that they lose all their originality.

Peer pressure can really cramp your style. Carl Gustav Jung spotted how restrictive it can be. He said that most people walk around as though they're wearing shoes that are too small for them. Ouch.

When you own your individuality, you shine

Don't let life hem you in. I want to inspire you to have the courage of your own convictions. When you own your individuality, you shine. And as Wilde put it, when you consider that everyone else is already taken, being yourself is an extremely sensible move.

Find your confidence

I have spent many years and expended far too much energy on apologizing. I am who I am and there is nothing I can do about that.

EMMA THOMPSON

It's very important to keep what confidence you have, no matter how dire the circumstance. You have to learn to shelter and protect it from the onslaught.

BETTE DAVIS

Confidence confuses people because they think it's all about serene certainty. It's not. Confident people are not always free of doubt. On the contrary, they may sometimes be full of doubts, and they know exactly what their flaws are. What makes the confident person stand out is that they embrace the flaws and the fear and get on with what they have to do. They realize that no one expects them to be perfect.

Kate Winslet recounts how she learnt to accept herself and how she found her confidence in the process.

Kate Winslet

Be who you are. *Everybody* has something special to offer. It took me a long time to find my own confidence as a person. It wasn't until I was sixteen or seventeen that I was able to start really feeling confident in myself.

Over the years there are a few people who have given me words of encouragement that have stayed with me. Emma Thompson took me under her wing on *Sense and Sensibility*. I was nineteen and she was thirty-five at the time. She was so brilliant. She always made me feel that it wasn't an accident that I had got that part. I so could not believe that I was there. I really thought somebody was going to walk up to me and say, 'I'm so sorry but when we made the phone calls after the audition we read the wrong name. You were the wrong girl.' Emma was just so great, telling me that I was the person they had wanted. Frankly she made me feel really good about being me. She was incredibly encouraging and complimentary and did give me the confidence to always try those things and to believe in myself.

When I was cast in *Eternal Sunshine [of the Spotless Mind]*, again I could not believe that I was being asked to play that part. I'd done so many period films and was a little bit stuck in corseted roles. I couldn't believe that director Michel Gondry wanted me to play a part that was nothing like anything I'd done before. To fully understand his vision I asked him, 'Why did you want me to play the part, why me, not X, Y or Z?' He just listed all the things that he had seen in me. Then, I got it. I felt very understood. It gave me the courage and confidence to do anything. It all comes from the inside.

He would say to me, 'Just try, just do it, just play. It doesn't matter if you look stupid.

I want you to look stupid.' It was such a release, talk about taking off the psychological lid. On day one of shooting the lid came right off and it never went back on, not even for a simmer. It was amazing, that feeling of, 'OK, lift the lid, girl! . . . Just take that lid off and leave it off.'

Look closely at the people you admire and you see that flaws make them more attractive, not less. When you accept this in *yourself*, you relax and you shine. As Alan Cumming puts it, 'Why be ashamed about being you?' Having a few flaws to balance your strengths makes you human.

Kate explained how she was struck by the horrible, confidence-sapping feeling of being the 'wrong girl'. This is impostor syndrome, and it's a real beast. If you've ever had the sense that someone was going to find you out, tap you on the shoulder and then escort you sharply out of the building, then you've experienced impostor syndrome. At least 50 per cent of my clients say that they feel it sometimes. The higher they rise in their careers the more it seems to occur. You'd be amazed how many people who seem to be sublimely confident and in charge, feel the nagging uncertainty and self-doubt of impostor syndrome.

Impostor syndrome causes you to shut down, screwing the

lid on tight. You fear saying or doing anything that will give you away as inadequate. You put up a front of confidence, which is brittle and tense, and makes people suspicious of what you are hiding. It's a vicious circle, because the more you close down, the less you contribute. Then people doubt you, and you trust yourself less. You have to eradicate impostor syndrome if you are to excel.

Understand that your uniqueness is as much about your flaws as your gifts

How do you overcome it? The secret is to understand that your uniqueness is as much about your flaws as your gifts. Your flaws give you texture and make you a three-dimensional human being. Those who love you see you as irreplaceable, not because you are perfect, but because you are *you*.

Accept yourself in the same way. Don't expect to be good at everything, no one is, it's freakish. So you can't sing? At least you're a great dancer. Bad at spelling? You're a whiz at problem-solving. Shy? Well at least you take in the details about people in conversation. Can't cook? You make a stunning cup of tea. Merely reminding yourself that you have something unique to bring to the party can be a great cushion of comfort when doubts flood in.

Why should it matter to know your flaws as well as your strengths? It gives you a clear-sighted perspective on exactly what you offer, and a better sense of how others see you. That self-knowledge brings humility. Carl Gustav Jung believed that when you can see your strengths and weaknesses clearly, you can stand at the centre of yourself. You don't have to pretend to be something you're not. So, how do you lift the lid in your own life?

First, take Alan Cumming's advice to 'understand your own power'. Know what it is, specifically, that you offer. If there's one thing you do really well, you can build your confidence from there.

Second, accept the things that you feel unsure about, as well as the things that are wonderful about you. Peter O'Toole calls this perspective 'consciousness of self'. It's the antidote to self-consciousness, because you develop perspective rather than anxiety. O'Toole was taught at the Royal Academy of Dramatic Art (RADA) that one must learn to recognize 'one's defects, one's strengths, one's weaknesses, one's powers, one's limitations, one's possibilities'.

Take this awareness into your life. Be as assiduous about your possibilities as your limitations. When you over-dramatize your possibilities you become grandiose. When you over-think limitations, you become defeated. Find the balance. Then, with the perspective that consciousness of self offers, be confident to hang on to your quirks. Rufus Sewell explains how.

Rufus Sewell

These days, I fight for my idiosyncrasies. I've tried to exist without them, thinking that people wanted me to part with them. Don't part too willingly with the very things that you need. Remember that what you offer are the things that make you specifically who you are, not what makes you like everybody else. Your oddities, the things that make you ridiculous, are exactly the things that make you human.

Keep holding on to your oddities. Trust what you see is blue, rather than what you imagine other people see as blue. Don't accept other people's description. Use your own. Don't take a short cut to what you imagine other people see as the truth. It becomes like a Chinese whisper, an impression of an impression of an impression. Sometimes the truth is a little bit quirky or difficult to explain. Try to avoid the mistake of the Chinese whispers, to ingratiate and second guess what you think is expected of you.

In those moments when you start worrying about, 'What do they see in me, what do they want?' just remind yourself that it's you, the very relaxed you, the you in front of the bathroom mirror, that people want. Don't throw the real you away, because you think people want something else. It's like when people go round scouting for extras on the street and they are delighted to find some really cool hippy kid. Then to their dismay the kid turns up on set the next day with white teeth and a suntan. Fight for your idiosyncrasies. Don't part too willingly with the very things that you need.

Try it. Hold on to your oddities. Trust that you offer something unique. Know that you are enough. Notice how it allows your confidence to bud and blossom. Remember Shirley Bassey's lyric: 'Life ain't worth a damn until you can say I am what I am.'

Never let the opinions of others become your opinion of yourself

All you have is who you are, all you have is your instinct and the second that gets rocked by someone else's judgement, it all starts to go wrong.

KATE WINSLET

I talk to a lot of women on my show, and often at about age thirty-nine or forty, they think, 'My God, I have become what everybody else wanted me to be . . . This wasn't my dream . . . How did I get here?' You start acting based upon others' definitions of who you are, and you just take that role in life.

OPRAH WINFREY

Opinions, opinions. Everyone has one. It's so much easier to have an opinion than to create something. Our culture is saturated with opinion from the informed to the idiotic. If you have an instinct to do something, you should trust it, and test it. Don't be blocked by what others think. In particular don't ever let people limit your horizons.

Many of us have inherited a rule book from friends and family. Some of the rules are useful, but more often than not you outgrow them. That's why standing out often involves breaking some of the old rules and politely rejecting restrictive opinions. The opinion that says you can't try a new career is there to be tested. Break the rule that says it's wrong to smile at the handsome stranger across the room. Flout the tradition that says you're shy and you can't make a speech.

Sarah Jessica Parker has had her share of success and the opinions that accompany it. She passed on what she's learned with a real warmth and generosity of spirit, even though, as she said, she's normally loath to give advice.

Sarah Jessica Parker

The ultimate goal, and this goes for everybody, is not to let other people's opinions of you become your opinion of yourself. You can put ten people in a room and they can be sequestered and not know you're listening and all of them will say something about who you are, none of which, at all, is the way you think of yourself. Imagine trying to adapt, as you go down that line, to every person's ideas. You would be a nobody. You'd come out without any point of view of who you are and no perspective of your worth.

Beyond that you need to recognize – and this is incredibly hard to do – what you feel good about, physically, mentally, intellectually and certainly emotionally.

How you figure out who you are is really important. Entrench yourself in your own identity. People are told 'do this' and 'you should look this way'. These things are not helpful, especially to a young person. You learn who you are by having disappointments and failures, as well as success. You learn by how your peers or your colleagues think of you, in terms of the respect they have for you because of the choices you make. Eventually you start charting your own course in a very deliberate way. But it takes a long time.

There's a whole part of our culture that says unkind things all day, every day. Everything is scrutinized and we're all on the internet talking about each other, writing blogs and columns; it's just an endless cycle of people's opinions and criticisms. When something hurtful is said about you, I don't think you get over it for a long time. I think you carry it with you and maybe it makes you more of who you are. Maybe you tell yourself I'm in good company, or it's par for the course, but it's still hard to forget. And you can go back to that place in a heartbeat and recall that feeling. For me, it's part of who I am, I bring it along with me, I drag it around behind me. I don't know how to pretend it didn't happen. It takes time and experience to be circumspect about that and be philosophical. It just can't affect what you do. It can be really sad, or it can be embarrassing, and you want to defend yourself, but you really cannot let it in too much. I can't. It would cut me off at my knees.

Sarah Jessica is absolutely right that you *cannot* pay too much attention to the opinions of others. Star quality is a galaxy away from that. Trust your instinct and set yourself free from tittle-tattle and the need for approval.

Legendary acting teacher Uta Hagen warned against the insidious pressure of the group. 'We must overcome the notion that we must be regular . . . We must learn to balk at this social dictum in order to enlarge our imagination and our use of self.' Ignore the sirens who say 'be like one of us', against your best instincts. Paying too much attention to them, Uta said, is the quickest path to mediocrity. Mediocrity says it all. It means, literally, that you are in the middle, 'media'. When you are lost in the middle of a crowd, it's near impossible to be outstanding. Take Uta's advice, and strike out on your own path.

Why is it so hard to shut out the opinions of others? When your self-worth is founded on the opinions of others, you can quickly become an approval addict. Doyenne of acting teaching Viola Spolin called it 'approval syndrome' and warned that it can creep like a weed into your life if you let it. 'Dictating and critiquing the way you do things, creating robot-like behaviour in you, with almost total loss of any insight.'

When people get hooked on approval it causes all the keeping-up silliness: hostility, envy, competitiveness, sarcasm and put-downs. Those who pay too much attention to what others about them think are often the most opinionated. They spend so much time criticizing and commenting on everyone else, that they don't create anything of their own. Approval addiction is hollow, because you've lost control of your own perceptions. Because it's so much easier to criticize than create, approval addiction is utterly anti-creative.

The antidote to approval addiction? Trust your instinct and keep your own counsel. If you don't depend on the opinions of the group they lose their power. It's no fun to criticize someone who doesn't need your approval. Sigourney Weaver says she's learned that fitting in is a great illusion. 'Women in particular have the idea that they're supposed to be perfect and that they're not and everyone else is . . . I think the truth is nobody fits in but everybody wants to.'

The next time you are told what to think, tune in to your instinct. If you feel excited, positive, at ease, take the advice. If the advice makes you feel sick, uncertain, doubtful, listen to your own instincts. *Trust your instinct* Keep checking in with what you feel and let that be your guide. If you know you can rely on your own gut, you don't need to take on board the opinions of others – unless, of course, it feels right.

Be careful who you listen to. When it comes to choosing *who* to listen to, be guided not by the many but by the very select few. Nothing brilliant was ever designed by committee. Find a trusted adviser who understands you. They are often ahead of you on a similar path, and have a sense of your dreams and ambitions, as well as an unromantic awareness of the obstacles you face. Know who your chosen few are and pay serious attention when they give advice.

As to the rest, expect negativity from the opinionated. Dali said that the true sign of success was the jealousy of the malcontents. Change frightens people, and you will always meet criticism when you have the courage to step out of line. Don't let it throw you if your instinct tells you you're on the right track. Susan Sarandon believes that the courage it takes is worth the fear, if it's for something you believe in. 'By definition you must be inappropriate if you are challenging the status quo.'

Dr Seuss summed it up perfectly: 'Be who you are and say what you feel, because those who mind don't matter and those who matter don't mind.'

Your charisma is in your calling

I've come to believe that each of us has a personal calling that's as unique as a fingerprint – and that the best way to succeed is to discover what you love and then find a way to offer it to others.

OPRAH WINFREY

Follow your bliss. If you are on your own path then things will come to you.

SUSAN SARANDON

Charisma is delightfully old-fashioned. In a world of spin and surface, charisma is about searching within, finding your talent and using it to do some good for the world. When you have a clear, passionate purpose you exude natural enthusiasm, which means, in Ancient Greek, 'filled with God'.

The secret to finding charisma is in *charis*, the Greek root of the word. It can be translated as 'gift'. Whatever your gift, if you can find a way to use it for the common good, you find your charisma.

Genuine charisma is charmingly immune to the ministrations of the spinners. You only have it when you do what you love. The open body language, the alive eyes, the rich warm voice and the passionate, expressive gesture, are not to be found in any charisma-by-numbers kit. A cheesy grin doesn't count.

Faking charisma actually makes you look a bit demented. It doesn't work when it's used for selfish or self-aggrandizing purposes, because without the glow of compassion, there is no charisma. The passionate activist always has so much more charisma than the 'on-message' politician, reciting the party line. Even though the politician has almost certainly been 'taught' how to do it.

Great actors know about charisma because they love what they do. Gael Garcia Bernal is going to share with you what he's learned about trusting his instinct and finding his passion. When you find your passion your star quality shines so bright it dazzles the world.

Gael Garcia Bernal

One thing that I say to myself, and I say to everyone, is: do what you enjoy. Be very sure of the things you're doing and why you're doing them. When it's fun you throw yourself into it without any holding back. Passion helps you. When you have passion, there's a glow of innocence which is quite pure and quite strong. It even scares some people, pushes them back, because it's not human to be so defenceless. But if you're inspired you can inspire others.

It's an art, finding out who you are and what you want. Who you are changes. It was the director Declan Donellan [founder of Cheek by Jowl and the writer of *The Actor and The Target*] who taught me that the important question for a role is 'Who do I want to be?' rather than, 'Who am I?' It gets to the heart of how transitory our state of being is. As the past is gone, and the present slips away, the future is really all we have. Asking 'Who do I want to be?' rather than, 'Who am I?' keeps you moving forward.

Then the art is to keep going until you feel that you are completely congruent, doing exactly what you need, exactly what you enjoy. If you don't yet know what that is, set yourself the challenge of finding out. It's instinct, not analytical, a gut thing. You can get an objective point of view after you've done it, after you've taken the decision. And if it doesn't feel right, you stop and say, this is not the right way, and you go the other way.

Whenever you believe in something and embark on the journey to find it, you always feel a little bit alone. Dreams are easily destroyed, but remember that when you're doing something for the common good, then there's an army behind you. They will always be there. When it's honest, you're doing something that people will connect with.

Put yourself in situations where you will grow and challenge yourself. Yes, it's daunting. Taking that step is kind of scary. It's always scary to say something truthful and honest. I think, even the people who do it are scared. You have to breathe in and take the step. You put it out there, you breathe in and then you just do it.

Passion is at the heart of charisma. Think of something that matters to you and notice how your voice changes, your eyes fill with energy, the lights go on. It's a feeling of happiness in the body that bubbles up like a good champagne. It's so different from the energy you have when you don't care. Then the bubbles go flat.

If you want to inspire others you must first be inspired yourself. Professor Richard Wiseman's research into charisma supports this. He found that charismatic people are particularly good at making others feel emotion strongly. Actors and orators have known, since the time of Aristotle and Horace, experts on rhetoric in the Ancient World, that whatever you want your audience to feel, you

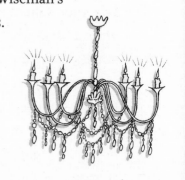

have to feel yourself. Charisma comes from feeling so strongly about something that others feel it, too. Will Smith recognizes it, saying that his presence comes from his love of what he does. 'That's infectious. It's something that you can't fake. And I think that the camera can feel that I'm happy doing what I do, and it's something that gets inside of people.'

If you want charisma, follow the principles that Gael has identified:

- **Find your purpose.** Do what you love. Passion is hard to fake. Outstanding people love what they do. If you think laterally you either have to make your passion pay, or organize your life so that there's room for your passion in your free time.

- **Live your values.** Your values are what you stand for. Write a list of what matters to you in life – these are your values. Values are trigger points, because when someone goes against your values, whether it's by being dishonest, hurting someone, or behaving unethically, you get angry. When you are in congruence with your values you feel that all is right with the world. If you feel sick, or ill at ease, respond to that. Charismatic people understand that if your values tell you not to do something, and you go ahead, then your whole system screams out the confusion. People read it in your eyes; they hear the uncertainty in your voice. You have to live in accordance with what you stand for if you are to demonstrate integrity, and to build trust. Integrity, after all, comes from the Latin word for whole.

- **Speak your mind.** If you don't feel congruent, speak out with sensitivity. It makes you far more effective because people feel you can be trusted. Professor Frank Bernieri at Oregon State University explains that we like people who communicate in an open, animated and expressive manner because we can read them more clearly. If you seem ill at ease or incongruent you lose our trust.

- **Take risks.** Charismatic people are passionate enough about their ideas to take risks, to make the scary phone call, to make the speech, to stand up for their beliefs. Safety is rarely charismatic, so if you want to stand out, be prepared to feel scared. Relish it, and tackle the fear step by step. If you have an instinct that something is right, trust your gift, breathe in and go for it. If it's meant to work, it will. If it doesn't, you've learned something useful.

Standing out is not about being perfect, or being approved of, or being the best. It's simply about making the best contribution you can make, with the resources that you have. When you take the brave step of trusting your instincts above the opinions of others, and living your values, you'll find that you start to shine in what you do. Passion is rare and powerful, because so many people are scared to take the risk. Decide *how you are valuable* rather than *how valuable you are*. Be brave enough to step forward and to be who you are – the results can be wonderful, for you and for others.

Your toolkit

- **Remember, no one else has ever been you before.** No one else will be again. It stands to reason that you have the best instinct on how to do things. So trust your gut, and get on with it.
- **Accept your flaws.** Get over not being perfect. No one else is.
- **Don't let the opinions of others become your opinion of yourself.** Trust only your chosen few, and don't get hooked on approval syndrome. Creating something original is so much more fun than being approved of by the herd.
- **Do the thing you love:** then you'll find that work is more fun than fun. That's a big part of charisma, and of success.

CHAPTER 2

Love Your Look

We cast a spell of allure by learning who we are,
and expressing ourselves . . . To me that's
bewitchingly attractive, that's glamorous.
That's finding your own magic.

SALMA HAYEK

Glamour is internal, the rest is window dressing.

JAMIE LEE CURTIS

How to Find Real Glamour

Have you ever wondered why some pretty people, when you meet them, seem unattractive to you? And why others, initially unprepossessing, can bewitch you within moments of your first encounter?

The attractiveness of the latter group has much to do with what the Quakers call 'the light inside', the glow of intelligence, openness and interest in others that puts shallow prettiness in the shade.

As the writer Umberto Eco explains, this magic, which he calls 'charm', has very little to do with how you look. 'Charm is something else, it can depend on a glance, on the way you move a finger. So Barbra Streisand has a horrible nose, but she has something else. There are other values, charm and sexiness.'

So, how does charm, this inner magic, work? You switch on your magic when you accept the way you look, rather than striving to meet impossible standards of aesthetic perfection. The off-switch for your magic is insecurity, competitiveness and self-consciousness. When you like yourself and exude confidence through your voice, the light in your eyes, the warmth of your smile and the way you hold yourself, you are transformed and illuminated from within.

The world of retail would prefer you not to know too much about charm. Insecurity is good for business, because you spend money to feel better about yourself. The paradox is that this very insecurity is exactly what kills your latent magic in the first place.

There's nothing wrong in wanting to look well turned out. Clothes, hair and shoes are wonderful if they make you feel good. But if deep down you lack trust in yourself they will simply highlight that. Beautiful shoes only work if you have the confidence to walk tall in them.

This emphasis on the importance of accepting how you look is why young actors at drama school wear 'blacks' – black movement clothes – and are banned from wearing make-up. Even mascara is frowned upon. Why? Great acting is about the actor's inner life and if a young actor is fixated on the externals they will never do good work.

You switch on your magic when you accept the way you look

This is why it's crucial that young actors accept their look, rather than constantly glancing in the mirror for approval. At the same time they are encouraged to get fit, to enjoy their physicality and to develop their voices. This is a brilliant combination, one which allows young actors to shine from within and to find a magic that is theirs.

Clearly Hollywood is the main culprit in creating impossible air-brushed standards. Yet, interestingly, it doesn't have lasting respect for actors who succumb completely to its pressures.

The clones have a short shelf-life, because they are very easily replaceable. The majority of actors with lasting careers are those who manage to resist the pressure to conform. Kate Winslet, Frances McDormand and Sarah Jessica Parker all understand that what really matters is finding their own style. They trust that if it feels right, it is right, rather than bowing to external pressure to look a certain way. They're going to help you do the same.

Act beautiful

You can act beautiful, like you can act crazy or sad . . .
When I started you'd have Maggie Smith . . . she wasn't
a great beauty and neither was Peggy Ashcroft, but when
they were playing beautiful women, they were stunning.

FELICITY KENDAL

A straight line in art is a cardinal sin, because the visual arts value irregularity. 'Acting beautiful' is the acting equivalent. It's about finding a beauty that revels in your *im*perfection, allowing you to enjoy the way you look. It is emphatically different from vanity, which is pure insecurity. Those who radiate charm aren't trying to show off or compete in the beauty stakes. They are comfortable in themselves. Their ease is exactly what gives them their glow.

The paradox is that because some models, who have conventional good looks, spend so much time amongst other similarly pretty creatures, often they develop the very insecurity that makes them bland, dull and unprepossessing to talk to. The more they fixate on external perfection, the duller they become. The pouting and posing makes for self-conscious and unenjoyable conversation.

Kate Winslet knows all too well the pressure to be 'perfect' and she's had the chutzpah to stand up and criticize the airbrushing and surgery cultures. She's going to explain why you have to get past your insecurities, and forget the search for perfection, if you want to radiate the self-acceptance that you need to 'act beautiful'.

Kate Winslet

When I was a little girl I was stockier than other kids. I was very sporty and I did a lot of dance, but I was a bigger child. I never felt attractive and that kind of thinking stays with you your entire life.

It's impossible not to have your own insecurities about how you look, to think, I've got more crows feet than I had a year ago or my brow is so furrowed these days. You mustn't get wrapped up in things that at the end of the day are just distracting and not important. You look at people and you can see it a mile off. I have to rein myself in because I get very enraged.

Those lines are there for a reason, they're there because you cried really hard, or you laughed so much last night. Those things should be treasured; you should be grateful for them. Those are the great marks of life. The one thing I've realized is that no woman I knew ever said to me, 'I'm so proud of my body'. No one said to me, 'I love my body'. I've started doing that – obviously not in a full-on way! I have all of these imperfections, the stretch marks and scars that make us who we are.

Rather than doing what you would instinctively do about a part of your body that you're insecure about, saying 'get off', or 'don't do that', I say, 'I know, isn't that great.' At least I'm instilling in both of my kids a sense of pride in their physicality.

Kate's right to warn against the slippery slope of insecurity. Worrying about how you look is an awful waste of time, especially since the likelihood is that you look better now than you will in ten years' time. You may as well enjoy it.

You have to know how to think yourself out of this insecurity. This is exactly what Edith Evans, the Dame of her day had to do one night at the Old Vic Theatre in London. She recounted the story to a group of students at the Royal Academy of Dramatic Art (RADA) of the night she had to overcome her own insecurities to go on stage as Cleopatra.

Getting ready in her dressing room one night, Dame Edith was struck by the debilitating thought that she just wasn't beautiful enough to play the 'Serpent of old Nile'. She knew that the self-consciousness would be damaging to her performance.

Rather than panic, and spin into insecurity, Dame Edith took control. Dame Edith knew that the answer was in her inner life. Cleopatra *didn't* have to look like a young Liz Taylor; but she *did* need the belief that she was irresistible to Mark Anthony. She willed herself, mind and body, into the allure she needed.

As she sat in her dressing room, she had to find the memory of another time when she had felt beautiful from within. She explained that she looked into the mirror and spoke out loud to her reflection. She spoke the words aloud: '*You are beautiful.*' She repeated the words a number of times, each time allowing the phrase to help her access a memory of feeling her own power as a woman. With the repetition of each phrase her voice carried more certainty, emphasis and conviction: '*You ARE beautiful.*' As she recounted this story to the students, she grew before their eyes from a delicate old lady into an elegant queenly beauty: her spine straightened, her eyes sparkled, the years dropped away.

If you want to be able to do this in your own life you need to understand what the great actor-director-teacher Michael Chekhov called 'the feeling of beauty'. Chekhov explained that, 'Everything has two sides, one that is right, and the other, which is a caricature . . . Beauty, when it becomes a primitive "showing off", is an obvious caricature of itself.' The dark side of beauty, the 'showing off', is the 'slippery slope'.

A lack of self-consciousness is the first requirement for accessing the feeling of beauty. The reason why Madonna cannot act well is because of her focus on the external. As a dancer she uses mirrors to create perfect external form, a kind of 'showing-off'. There are always curtains to pull over mirrors in dance studios at drama schools. Why? You need mirrors to learn ballet but they are absolute anathema to great acting. Acting requires that you let go of self-consciousness to become what Stanislavsky called 'self-forgetful'. You focus on what you are doing, rather than the impression you are making.

How do *you* create a feeling of beauty? Michael Chekhov advised that, as Dame Edith did, you have to connect inside yourself. You have to find a place of comfort, as Kate suggested, in your physicality. You have to live as much in your body as you do in your head. Chekhov's advice is clear: 'Start with simple movement, and listen within you to the pleasure, the satisfaction, your limbs experience while moving . . . Move at first slowly, sifting away everything but the natural born feeling of beauty.'

The more you connect into your inner life, via your breath, and your awareness of your body, the more *sensual* you become, because you are tuned into your *senses*. Moreover it's a sensuality that is yours. It doesn't seek the approval of others. Michael Chekhov explains, 'A noble satisfaction will arise in you if you are on the right track; not the satisfaction a person may experience when they want to please someone who is looking at them.' When you change how you look to please someone else, then the only possible way to make yourself feel better is to show off. But the approval you seek is hollow, because it's outside. It becomes a fix. When you look the way you do, because it feels right, then you ooze a self-confident glamour that is utterly yours.

When you look the way you do, because it feels right, then you ooze a self-confident glamour that is utterly yours

Watch a cat or dog stretching and you can see a total unselfconscious immersion in the movement. As an adult you can relearn to move with the same attention to the sensation of movement. Aldous Huxley called this unselfconscious simplicity 'grace', seeing it in the pure connection that young children and animals have to their being, unblocked by insecurity. You see it in adults when they really laugh. Everyone is beautiful when they are genuinely laughing and not thinking about how they are looking to others. When you really embrace and enjoy the full range of your physical self, then you start to hook into the power of 'the feeling of beauty'.

Define yourself

*When I started, I knew I didn't fit any visual that
anyone was going to lie down and take their clothes
off about. If you come in and you're imitating everyone
else, you get swept away in the game. But if you're
coming as one unto yourself, they can't replace you;
they can only try to get somebody who's like you.*

WHOOPI GOLDBERG

*Have the courage to be yourself.
The courage to be unique.*

SALMA HAYEK

It was the individualistic and glamorous Coco Chanel who
said that if you want to be irreplaceable, you need to be different. This independence of mind is the well-spring of real
glamour, and it does take courage in a world where, increasingly, everyone looks, and sounds the same. One aspect of
this glamour is making your own choices, looking the way
you look because it feels right, not because someone else tells
you to. All that matters is that the decisions you make come
from a trust in yourself, not a loathing enforced from outside.

Sarah Jessica Parker and Frances McDormand will tell you more about trusting this instinct, and making the decisions they made to avoid surgery, because it felt wrong to them.

Sarah Jessica Parker

Even though I'd been working for a number of years by the time I was twenty-one or twenty-two, there were people who, if I had allowed them, would have changed me in a lot of ways. Physically, they would have encouraged and counselled me to do things to cosmetic myself that (I'm so grateful for now) I just didn't feel comfortable with.

It's so hard to hear comments like: she's not pretty enough to play that part, she should pluck her eyebrows, she should fix her nose, her hair should be straight. But you really can't let that kind of stuff in. I was hardly a confident young woman but somehow I trusted my natural instinct not to change myself. It just seemed anathema. I would encourage young people to not be influenced by others saying things like, 'I can't believe you think she's pretty.' Well, pretty is subjective, just as art is subjective, smell is subjective and taste is subjective.

Frances McDormand

Sometimes you just are too this and not enough that. You can be too short, too thin, too dark, too anything. As a woman, I have always judged myself harshly against whatever model of beauty that has been offered at the moment. In auditions I started to realize that what we all had in common was being The Other.

I've always attempted to make the ones hiring me see that I was the one they needed to tell their story because I was *not* like anyone else. I've made not fitting in desirable. I think that all the characters I've created, for better and sometimes for the worse, have that in common.

The profession of acting has always been linked to cosmetic looks. This is the unfortunate and, I believe, dangerous element of the profession. I peruse fashion magazines to get an idea of what's expected of me and the women I play. The ideals have changed radically over the thirty years I've been working.

Age and gravity have finally given me a better perspective of myself. I sincerely believe that changing oneself through plastic surgery is professional suicide. I am being dramatic, of course. That's my job. I think that to freeze the tools of expression in one's face or to alter the map that one's life has created there is like a pianist chopping off their fingertips.

The faces I've witnessed change in the past few years can only be employed in a story about a mutant tribe of people who can only identify who they trust by the same nose, chin or frozen expression. It's an epidemic that I hope to expose. Once again, I hope to corner the market on the roles available to a woman over fifty who has not done anything to her face but pluck her eyebrows.

Glamour originally meant 'magic'. It originated in the Latin word *grammatica* (grammar) – which came to mean the occult in the Middle Ages. Glamour is about finding your own grammar, just as Sarah Jessica Parker and Frances McDormand have suggested. It's about discovering your individual way of thinking, moving, speaking, dressing. Real glamour can be found in the instinctive, unselfconscious flair of a gesture, the arch of an eyebrow, or the purr of a voice. It is found in the sixty-year-old with attitude, as much (if not more) as the eighteen-year-old. Just look at Vivienne Westwood and Meryl Streep.

There's no right or wrong when it comes to defining your look. Everyone has the absolute right to make their own choices, but it's worth noting that Sarah Jessica Parker and

Frances McDormand have found success and longevity without giving in to the external pressure to look a certain way.

There's no right or wrong when it comes to defining your look

They have followed what felt right to them, trusting their instinct. The confidence and sparkle that this gives them makes them great examples of Jamie Lee Curtis' principle that 'glamour is internal and the rest is window dressing'. When you like your look – without self-consciousness – you radiate a confidence that is enormously attractive.

Salma Hayek explains, 'Glamour . . . no longer means simply aspiring to be an object to be looked at, a decoration. For me personally, glamour can mean being strong, professional, elegant, compassionate . . . A true sense of style . . . is understanding the best way to present yourself – because you feel completely comfortable. It is being a participant in the world by contributing to it. It's a whole, well-rounded experience and it's something to experience completely.'

Observe how the truly glamorous are at ease in themselves, and in their look. Tune in to your senses, your sensuality; notice when you feel good about yourself and when you don't. Start making active choices to define yourself, rejecting external prescriptions *if they don't feel right*. It's the only path to real, and enduring glamour, what Salma calls having a voice and confidence of your own.

Your toolkit

- **Glamour is internal and the rest is window dressing.** To illuminate your look from within, think these three thoughts to yourself: You are beautiful. Someone loves you. You have a secret. Try it – it works.
- **Find your voice.** Real glamour is in finding your unique style. The best way to do it is to – literally – find your voice. Your voice is the most powerful signal to others of your rich inner life. It's one of the most attractive elements about you, and because it's a muscle, you can maintain it as you age. Try Roger Love's *Voice* CD, which accompanies his book *Set Your Voice Free*; www.rogerlove.com. Patsy Rodenburg and Barbara Houseman both write clear, practical, accessible books on voice. You will find the best voice coaches via good drama schools.
- **Get into your body.** Glamour is about inner life expressed in outer form. Good actors are in touch with their bodies. They move well, and it can give them real presence. Get in touch with your body and you become more sensuous, and sensual. A simple daily practice is to meditate with your back against the wall. Gently release the back of your

head into the wall, dropping the chin. Feel your neck and jaw release. Feel your shoulder blades drop, moving closer together, and your collarbones moving away from each other. Do this every day and your body will start to find a lovely open alignment again. If you want to work in more detail on the grace of your movement, the best place to start is what actors are taught: Alexander Technique, Feldenkrais, Yoga and Pilates. All are well worth doing, as classes or one-to-one if you can afford it. You must see a qualified teacher and you can find out more at www.feldenkrais. com, www.alexandertechnique.com, www.yoga.com, www. iyengar-yoga.com and www.pilates.com.

CHAPTER 3

Enjoying Parties

I usually feel that time should be entertained. There is actual work in keeping groups moving forward. I'm perfectly willing to give up control, but somebody has to be in control. It's no good if nobody's asking, 'Who wants wine?' Maybe they'll get wine or they won't, maybe they'll get cheese or maybe not. It's the real version of 'The show must go on'.

GEORGE CLOONEY

How to Sparkle, Flirt and Have Fun

A party can be a joy in which you celebrate great friendships and forge new ones. It can also be an agony in which your every fear is confirmed. If you usually feel the latter sensation, then it's worth learning to enjoy parties.

There are two main reasons why parties can feel so daunting. The first is introversion. A surprising number of well-known actors are introverts. They include Clint Eastwood, Michelle Pfeiffer and Helen Mirren. Introverts are great performers, but they use up most of their energy to survive it. Parties are a form of performance and they are a particular challenge for the introvert. All that noisy chatting can wear you out and leave you feeling drained. Extroverts rarely dread a party in quite the same way, because they recharge in groups of people.

The second reason for party phobia is shyness. It may surprise you that many actors are shy, but acting gives them a way to hide in plain sight. They find going to a party much harder than hiding behind a character on stage. Shyness is different from introversion. When you are shy you feel incredibly self-conscious around others. You worry enormously about being judged and found wanting. Going to a party can make you feel the anxiety of being in the spotlight, with all the accompanying symptoms that actors suffer before going on stage.

Acting teaches actors skills to deal with introversion and shyness in professional situations. They have some great tips and tricks to help you survive the melee and face your fears of social performance. It's worth making these skills work for you. Only the churlish would inflict their antisocial instincts upon others. When you learn how to enjoy the throng of a party, you can benefit in all sorts of unexpected ways. You open yourself up to the magic of serendipity – you just never know who you might meet.

Psych yourself up

You can truly change your attitude by acting a different way. [On Enchanted*] I was pooped, in no mood to be the cheerful princess. I often thought of that line in* Mary

Poppins *at the beginning of 'A Spoonful of Sugar': 'In every job that must be done, there is an element of fun, you find the fun and snap, the job's a game.' I still sing that to myself. I am that corny, it's true.*

AMY ADAMS

The universal spark . . . Strike it, light it. When all the energy became boxed, so to speak, and it couldn't get out, then I just didn't come off. I was always very aware of whether I was boxed or fluid. Take a bath . . . cold . . . hot . . . relax. How's the motor running?

KATHARINE HEPBURN

Waltzing into rooms and dazzling everyone is a real performance skill. Even the apparently gregarious often have to gear themselves up for the hurly-burly of a big event. If your preference is more about being tucked up in bed than dancing the night away, acting can help. The solution to party phobia is to be found in the toolkit that propels an actor on stage (or on set) to give a wonderful performance, regardless of how they feel. A professional actor always finds the energy, no matter how tired they may be feeling.

Actors are experts at 'turning the lights on', even when their batteries feel run down. The 'half' is a sacrosanct time for actors in theatre. It's the half hour before the show starts.

The stage manager gives them their 'calls', counting down to 'beginners' call' when the first actors on stage must be ready to go. In that 'half' the actor pulls mind and body into a focused, potent state. They may have walked into the theatre exhausted a couple of hours before, but they will always walk on stage with focused energy. There are no excuses for the professional.

Film acting also requires the ability to manage energy. Film days are long, often eighteen hours. The actor may not have much to do for long periods, but when they are called, they must be energized and focused. Philip Seymour Hoffman explains, 'It is a marathon with small sprints during the day that is part of a long race. You really are gauging how much energy to use over a period of time so that you conserve energy . . . You must decide when to really go for it and when to pace yourself.'

Understanding how to pull yourself together at a moment's notice is powerful. If you've had a long day it will help you to get geared up for the energy demanded of you at a noisy party. Kate Winslet talks here about how she takes control of her state when she least feels like it, and most needs it.

Kate Winslet

On those days where you wake up and you think, 'I'm fat, I'm ugly, I have spots on my face and my bum', you have to play tricks on yourself. Don't doubt yourself, even when that hideous ugly devil voice inside you starts to tell you, 'I've got the wrong shoes on and I shouldn't even be here.' You have to trick yourself out of it. You just have to close your eyes, sit in a quiet corner, make yourself think you're great. In your darkest most terrifying moments when you have zero confidence, sometimes there is no one else who is going to tell you. If you don't walk through the door with confidence then you're not going to give the best of yourself. You won't have the courage. When you walk into that room all your confidence can just leave you behind, stay in the door frame. It's an unbelievably tricky balance you have to find, walking in, being confident, grounded, standing on your own two feet, not embarrassed, not afraid, nothing to lose.

You only have yourself to rely on at the end of the day and whilst being taught things is incredibly helpful, when the chips are down, it's you and your private little toolkit. If you can't access that toolkit for yourself then you have nothing. It's about using things from your life, the painful bits and the happy bits, that are forming you as a person and drawing on them as an actor. It's so much about courage. It's 50 per cent skill and 50 per cent courage and confidence.

Kate shows that actors know exactly how to use the toolkit to pull themselves up by the bootstraps when they feel themselves fading. The fact is this: you are in sole charge of your state of mind. You can use the fact that you feel rubbish as an excuse to make everyone else feel rubbish. Or you can be bigger than that. You can psych yourself up to be great company and make others feel good, too.

Kate has told you that, when the chips are down, it's just you and your toolkit. Actors have to have a toolkit to allow them to adjust their energy, because they must be able to perform when required, no matter how they are feeling. John Hurt explains, 'The business of being a professional is doing it even when you don't feel like it. You can't walk out on stage and say, "Sorry, I've had a bad day. Can we send the understudy out instead?" A professional can access concentration even when you don't think you can, when you're not feeling like it . . . You need to find a way to breathe deeply, to will yourself into the right mood. You have to know how to switch it on and off.'

It is exactly this ability to will yourself into the right mood that is an essential part of your psyching-yourself-up toolkit.

You take an active role in how you feel, rather than being subject to the vagaries of your emotion. Parties, because they are a real social performance, and because they often come at times when we are worn down and ready for a holiday, are the perfect place to test out your skill.

So, how do you psych yourself up? If you are to be able to change your state at will, you have to be in tune with your energy. Tune in to how you are feeling. This involves putting your attention in your body, as well as your brain. Katharine Hepburn called it checking how the motor was running. If you feel physically tired, like an actor, your best bet is to warm up physically, to go for a walk, run, do yoga. Or just jump around the house to music. If you're feeling frazzled, then you need to centre your energy, relax your shoulders and calm your breathing. Take a bath, listen to music, read a book. Diagnose exactly how you are feeling and then prescribe the perfect physical or psychological remedy. Sometimes what you want and what you need are not the same thing. If you are shattered, avoid slumping on the sofa. Actors rarely lie down just before a show. The bed in the dressing room is fine earlier on in the day, but if you need energy you need to move, to get the blood circulating. Once you lie down you slow down.

A very important tool in the toolkit is what acting calls 'emotion memory'. The technique comes from the work of

Stanislavsky and was one of the pillars of his early system. It's simple – you use the memory of a response to an event to release an emotion inside you. Stanislavsky was fascinated by how emotion memory could help his actors. He realized they could also use it to inhabit character. The system he developed has influenced actors ever since. In 1950 Lee Strasberg based the Method on Stanislavsky's work. Marlon Brando, Al Pacino and Marilyn Monroe all trained at Strasberg's Studio in New York.

Emotion memory is even better for life than it is for acting. An actor has to transfer their own memory to the world of their character, which is a little circuitous. You can use *your own memory* to rev you up direct from the source. It's your own personal storehouse of emotion for you to access whenever you want. Should you wish, you can choose to feel good at any time.

Try it. Take love. If you have ever fallen in love, your brain has stored that memory. Take a moment to go back in time to that moment. Visualize the face of your beloved, the place where you fell in love; see the details around you; picture the colours; inhale the smells; feel the temperature that day; visualize and feel what you were wearing; hear the sound of their voice; listen to the music that was playing; remember what was said.

You will discover that one of the details triggers the big

release of wonderful emotion. For a moment you are there again, as the positive memory fills you with the feeling of love. Your physiology responds to the good feeling. As far as your brain is concerned you are back in love again.

The beauty of emotion memory is that each time you re-access the memory, you can feel the same way again. The memory of falling in love changes the way you feel now. Actors also call it affective memory, because it *affects* you. To wake you up for your night out, remember the best party you've ever been to. Visualize it, see the details clearly and feel the rush fill you with energy once more.

Scientists have discovered that emotion memory is more than a drama technique. In fact Stanislavsky had first come across the notion that memory can positively affect us in the work of the French experimental psychologist Theodule Amand Ribot. Ribot found that patients reliving happy memories recuperated quickly. Recent research in the *American Journal of Cardiology*® backs this up. Scientists found that positive emotions boost everything from immunity to mental clarity, via the nervous system. In modern times, Stanislavsky has been proved right to the extent that the effect of the mind on the body is now a whole new science – that of psychoneuroimmunology (PNI).

So, back in the real world, when and how should you use emotion memory in your own life? The technique can make a real difference where you have to be on show and don't feel like it. It's a pleasant way to pull yourself together. When you'd rather be anywhere else, make yourself feel better by remembering a time where you were cheerful. Let it affect you in the now and feel your mood change. You may need to practise accessing the memories, as the more you bring them into your attention, the easier they are to recall. The more you use a neural connection, the faster it becomes.

You can also use 'sense memory' which is similar to emotion memory, but relies on the senses rather than your emotions. Instead of remembering a time in your life to release an emotion, with sense memory you visualize something that triggers a visceral sensation. So if you visualize a hot sun, or remember the feeling of great heat on your skin, the sound of waves on a beach, you can relax into a lovely holiday feeling, even if you're on the bus. If you visualize a hug, or remember the feeling of someone's arms around you, you feel comforted. Actors have some great memory tricks to jumpstart a good feeling. The best of all is to think of a 'naughty thought'. It gives you a mischievous sparkle, helping you get into 'camera out' mode, where you are extrovert, smiling and open, rather than 'camera in' where you lack sparkle because your mind is focused on your insecurities. You always have the choice.

Conquer your nerves

I'm a nervous wreck going into a crowded room . . .
I suppose I've built up a kind of veneer so that
I'm able to get through it all.

LAUREN BACALL

I was incredibly shy when I was little, outside of my
family group. So it's always been not a terribly natural
thing for me to feel comfortable walking into a
big room of people. But I'm trying to overcome it,
because it seems so self-centred.

GLENN CLOSE

The moment when you walk into a crowded room, and all eyes turn to you, can feel daunting. The secret to conquering your nerves is to take control of your *body*. You must train the butterflies fluttering in your stomach to fly in formation.

Dame Helen Mirren is going to help you with this. She has reigned at the Oscars, one of the most nerve-racking knees-ups in the world, with twenty-two million people watching her every move.

I'd been struck when I watched the footage of Helen at the Oscars by how calm and confident she looked. I asked what advice she has for channelling that calmness and confidence at the moments when you least feel like it and most need it.

Helen Mirren

I'm not gregarious or an exhibitionist . . . going to the bar after the show can be torture. I hate being looked at. From my perspective being in character allows freedom. But in my job you have to meet people constantly and deal with people you don't know. It can be torture. I was always very uncertain. I had panic attacks. I used to get very nervous. I'd feel ill, my hands would shake, get the sweats, the whole thing. I was incredibly nervous. It was very difficult on the first day's rehearsal having to walk in.

In general it's important *not* to act it, not to pretend. You have to be yourself and it can take you years to find out how to do this. If you're in a place of terror it's useful to drop the voice consciously and keep the shoulders low and open. I was taught by a policewoman at Holloway, don't fold your arms, stay open, keep your arms relaxed. Of course it's the hardest thing for women to do, and it's the ultimate acting problem, not knowing what to do with your hands. Guys are lucky because they can put their hands in their pockets. It's such a hard thing to let your arms drop, but it's so important to be open and relaxed. It was a great tip.

I've noticed that women have a tendency to speak over each other whereas men interrupt, but they listen. I'd advise women to speak loud, firmly use a low tone – demand to be heard. It's important to be able to talk loudly and keep the tone low. Often I hear women in noisy environments like clubs, the tone goes up and the voice gets shrill and high, much higher than it needs to be. The shrill quality is unpleasant, it sounds like noise. It's about learning to use the voice so that you can speak loudly and using the diaphragm, so that you can drop the voice. When the voice is lower it's easier to listen to.

Everyone feels shy and ill at ease when faced with the prospect of a daunting event. Nerves are good, they show that you care. And, as Helen shows you, you can cope with nerves if you take control of the body. Her advice is tried and tested and, like an actor's training, it is practical.

So, how do you make it look like you are poised under pressure? Acting training works on the principle that the mind and body work as one system, the 'psycho-physical'. The simple act of dropping your shoulders can shift you over from shyness to serenity. Marianne Williamson, the US spiritual teacher, puts it beautifully, 'It is easier to act your way to a new way of thinking than to think your way to a new way of acting.' If an actor feels scared they warm up, relaxing body and breath to get them past the fear. They trick themselves out of it. Katherine Hepburn described how she learned to get over her fears of acting on the stage. She said that nobody must ever know how terrified you are. 'You've got to be absolutely cool, although you may be dying inside.' Her advice on *how* to do it echoes Marianne Williamson: 'If you want a quality, act as if you already have it.'

Laurence Olivier had two rules when he got nervous: 'relax your feet' and 'always have more breath than you need'. I'm also a fan of the great Bette Davis' trick of pausing in the door frame for a moment. Stanislavsky called it the 'moment of orientation'. You see actors do it as they come on stage. It's that tiny pause where you connect with the room and your public. It gives you time to compose yourself, take in the room, and let the room notice you.

Helen's tip about dropping your shoulders is the first step to taking Olivier's advice. It gets the breath low, where it is when you're relaxed. Glenda Jackson, Oscar-winning actress and Member of Parliament, has a great physical tip to help you. She says a friend at the Royal Ballet would say, 'Display your diamonds, display your diamonds. The idea is that you've got this fantastic necklace so show it off.' Don't stop there, give yourself an imaginary crown, too, as it helps you lengthen the neck and look relaxed and swan-like. Then the best way I know to remember to breathe is to imagine a lovely smell in the room that you want to inhale fully, silently and deeply.

When it comes to keeping your voice low and gentle, relaxing your shoulders is extremely helpful. Make sure that you are also relaxed in the neck and jaw. Any tension in your body will affect your voice, and as Helen has told you, shrieking is to be avoided. Kathleen Turner explains, 'I meet women who you think are very glamorous . . . and then they open their mouth and their voice is so annoying and off-putting.' A tense voice is hard to listen to. A little joyful singing in the shower is a great way to relax and get the voice warm. Why joyful? Because when you're having fun you release fully, and that's the secret to a wonderful voice. It's open, rather than clamped down.

It's well worth developing your voice, by learning to sing, or taking lessons with a good voice coach. Research shows that people are perceived as intelligent (and sexy) if they speak in a low, strong and clear voice. The film critic Kenneth Tynan said the defining feature of the movie stars Lauren Bacall, Katharine Hepburn and Ava Gardner was that they all had low voices.

The most important element of a good voice is that it has ease. The voice, because it's supported by your breath, improves exponentially when you stand well, breathe low and relax your throat, jaw and tongue.

Don't get into the trap of pushing your voice down so that it sounds like hard work. *If it feels forced and artificially low, it isn't working.* Helen is encouraging you to speak from a low, relaxed place, where you laugh from. It gives you a calm gravitas, which many an actor has worked hard to achieve.

And if, even after relaxing your shoulders and feet, breathing the butterflies into formation, displaying your diamonds, you still feel nervous, Jenny Agutter has a wonderful psychological tip to get you through the door of the party. Her success with *The Railway Children* meant that as a young girl Jenny had to attend many daunting parties. She says that she was given some invaluable advice. 'When I was young, my mother taught me that if I was nervous I should go in with the idea that I had to leave in half an hour. If you're thinking, "I've only got half an hour", it stops you doing the "stuck in a corner" thing. You're only there for half an hour so you can enjoy it and talk.' Try it, it really works!

The integrity of real charm

When I was ten or eleven years old, my dad said, 'Look people in the eye when you talk'. I remember that really specifically, allowing them to be human beings. It humanizes all of us . . . I once had lunch with a movie producer who was completely dismissive and rude to our waiter, which told me all I needed to know about him . . . I'm in a position where he wants to be nice to me, since he needs something from me. But what happens if I'm not in that position any more? If he treats everyone else dismissively, he'll treat me dismissively.

GEORGE CLOONEY

True charm is a very democratic star quality. Charming people treat everyone they meet with respect and interest. The test of a charming person is how they talk to the waiter, rather than how they talk to their boss.

The heart of true charm is about seeing that everyone is unique and fascinating, the shy person at the canapés, the waiter on the first night of a new job, or your eighty-year-old neighbour. Genuinely charming

The heart of true charm is about seeing that everyone is unique and fascinating

people work on the principle that everyone deserves to be given their full attention. It is the antidote to the plague of BlackBerry-checking, clock-watching and over-the-shoulder-gazing that makes you feel unwelcome when you are on the receiving end. Life is often a power transaction and charming people allow others to share the power. They don't need to make others feel small to hoist themselves up.

Here Alan Cumming talks about the openness and interest in others that makes for real charm.

Alan Cumming

The people who have the most energy, spirit and the most *joie de vivre* are the most fun to be around. They're open – they don't have cynicism in the same way that a child doesn't. They're not children, but they have a childlike quality in that they are looking out to the world and are not standing on the back foot.

I really think that's the most attractive quality, to feel like you can go into any situation and take part, not feeling like you don't belong in certain places. I'm thinking about Ian McKellen; we've been in the most crazy disparate situations together, and we just get on with people. It's great when someone has that quality of being able to talk to anybody. I remember my granny being like that.

When I have a party I invite all my friends. I don't separate them. You know that thing where people are nervous because their friends from all different parts of their lives are there, and someone's going to offend someone else. I think they should all be able to get on with each other. I don't understand it sometimes when people aren't able to bring their friends together because they all enrich your life in some way. It's good to have them all.

It does vary according to your mood . . . there are times when you're not feeling so good and you're not feeling so attractive. You just have to let it happen. You're either going to have to deal with it and have a laugh, or go home.

If you're feeling uncomfortable with someone you're talking to, the best way to view it is that some people take a bit more work. There are times when I'm chatting to someone and I think we're not going to be able to make a connection, perhaps they're not feeling it for whatever reason, or maybe they lack openness and confidence. It's not the end of the world. You just move on.

Remember that you don't have to tell everyone every aspect of yourself all the time. It's an important thing to learn to be confident enough to let people come to you. It used to be that whenever I met someone, I'd be [at high speed], 'This is me and this is who I am . . . I think this . . . but I really feel like this.' And then I thought [slows down], 'How boring. If they can't be bothered to find out, then I'm not a little puppy going round trying to be liked by everybody all the time. I will be myself, and then gradually people will discover about me.'

It's important, because you can feel this pressure, especially when you're young, to try to say who you are, encapsulate yourself every time you meet someone new or go into a new situation. You can become boring, because you take up such a lot of time and energy doing that and also you just have to have the confidence that stuff about you will come out, by just having a normal conversation. You don't have to do your resumé and all your interests and opinions. It's more interesting just to be yourself. You don't have to show it – it's there.

Charm is about being open and attentive to others, rather than worried about how you are coming across. As Alan's told you, you have to ditch your self-consciousness. The 'spotlight-effect' in psychology says that no one else really notices the moments that you cringe at, so it's best not to worry too much. Extend yourself: open out your focus of attention, as actors do on stage, to take in the room. You notice who is comfortable, who needs another drink, who needs bringing in to the conversation.

The lightness and *joie de vivre* that Alan described is so important. Introverts often forget to smile, or show response. They are listening, but their focus is so internal that they forget to signal it. This can make them seem unapproachable and cold. Then they wonder why no one wants to talk to them at parties, and the circle gets more vicious.

If people sometimes have to remind you to smile, it helps to let go of all the things you're mulling on, and find a child-like delight in what's going on around you. This focus on the outside world is what Cate Blanchett calls 'turning the lights on'. It's a way for the introvert to project their energy out-wards, so that other people can share it. You can imagine bathing others in your energy, rather than conserving the light inside. You become a lighthouse, rather than a house with all the shutters closed. When you 'turn the lights on' you respond more with your eyes, you smile more, and your attention focuses outwards.

This warmth and lightness helps others to lighten up, too. Stanislavsky called it 'communion'. 'You experience an emotional state, and you make others, with whom you are in communion, feel the same.' Scientists at the Institute of HeartMath in Colorado have discovered there's a physiological reason why genuine warmth and positivity have such a good effect on others. When they compared electrical activity, the signals between one person's heart and another's brain had a measurable effect on each other. It's been described as 'heart-brain synchronization'.

Don't even consider faking charm. Faked charm is

switching on the outer signifiers of charm, the smile, the eyes, without the honest belief that others are important. Faked charm's spotlight is used only for those who can help. It leaves you cold when it's switched off. It looks weird, at best cheesy, at worst disingenuous and manipulative. Don't do it. Stanislavsky was critical of people who fake the connection, calling it 'pale imitations' of real communion. We all know the difference between the person who really engages and makes you feel great, and the person with the fixed smile going through the motions. Stanislavsky talked about their 'veiled eyes' as they think about something else and pretend to be interested. Not charming, but weird.

Don't even consider faking charm

Help others feel at ease

There are some simple and genuine ways to help others feel more at ease in social situations. It's said that George Clooney greets new people as if they're an old friend he's being re-introduced to. It switches on the emotion memory of being with someone you value. 'Hi!' The ice breaks instantly. Audrey Hepburn put it perfectly, 'For beautiful eyes look for the good in people.' It instantly helps you see them as unique.

Your smile naturally widens and your eyes crinkle up – it's called a 'Duchene smile' and it's something you can't fake. If you greet people with genuine warmth, both of you benefit from the warmth and pleasure it generates.

A great way to open up to others is to be curious about them. Then, as Alan reminded you, you have to talk less, which is usually the sign of the socially adept. Find people fascinating, let them talk, and your charm blossoms. Asking questions, taking an interest, makes you a brilliant conversationalist.

A great way to open up to others is to be curious about them

If you are shy at parties it's good to have two or three things to bring into conversation. Shyness is contagious, and however mundane and small-talky the thing you say, most people are so grateful to connect that they just don't mind. Be careful though. I hate it when people interrupt with their piece, it's a charm killer. Nerves are often the cause but it makes for jerky, uncomfortable conversations. Don't do it. Let people finish their thought fully. Stanislavsky told his actors, 'Trust your eyes . . . Observe each other constantly and you will always guess when one finishes a sentence or completes a thought.' The wonderful thing about charm is that when you act as if other people are fascinating, you become fascinating to them.

Flirting

Flirting is a natural extension of charm and great flirting is an essential part of life. It shouldn't be reserved for the game of finding a mate, because it makes so much of life more fun. It is all about the unabated pleasure in someone else's company and the sheer delight of making others feel great, bathing them in the sunlight of your undivided attention, tickling them with your interest. It's a gorgeous gift to give in a solipsistic society, and great flirts do it because they love people and they love the banter.

Great flirts know how to really see someone

What really makes this work is that great flirts know how to really *see* someone. They see what makes you different and special, and they share their appreciation of it with you. And at the same time they let you know, because they are at ease, that this is playful, not pushy. It's about the pleasure of a moment of mind-connection and it's devastatingly attractive. It creates a delightful sense of, 'I'm fantastic, you're gorgeous, the world is wonderful.' They make you feel like the time you are having with them is special and memorable to them. You feel funny, charming, unique and thoroughly glad to be alive.

To find this pleasure in others you have to have first found a sense of completeness and happiness in who you are. When you become playful and positive about life, you are able to give attention to others. It's so much more life-affirming than the desperation which drags others down. A great flirt boosts others with appreciation and admiration, giving them the experience of how it feels to be seen, admired and desired. If you could bottle it, it would be a worldwide bestseller.

Parties are a performance. When you realize that, you harness your energy, overcome your nerves, and turn the lights on. You become the adept party-goer you have always admired from afar. And, at the end of the night, as Cate Blanchett was taught by her teacher at drama school, you turn the lights off when you go home. Even A-list actors don't have to shine all the time.

Your toolkit

- **Manage your energy.** If you feel exhausted, do something about it. Check in with how you're feeling: Tired? Stressed? Shy? Then prescribe the right strategy to get your motor running. If you feel tired, don't lie down – get moving. If you need to calm down – have a bath. Then use emotion memory, the memory of a great party, or sense memory, the memory of a good feeling, to change the way you feel.

- **At the entrance of the party** Stand tall. Display your diamonds. Relax your shoulders and feet so you feel grounded and at home. Give yourself more breath than you need. Go in as if you've only got half an hour, so you make the most of it.
- **Treat everyone as a friend** Imagine that new people you meet are long-lost friends. Ask questions and listen more than you speak. It's the golden rule.

CHAPTER 4

Be Yourself
but Better

*How do we escape who we are? I think going to college,
I felt freer. I loved the clean slate. I wasn't known as
the sort of nerdy, studious girl . . . I needed that
expansion from a very conservative little town.*

JOAN ALLEN

*We look for the ordinary rather than the extraordinary
in our daily lives and so the explorations of ourselves
become smaller and of less importance as we go along.
We pigeonhole and characterize our very behaviour until
our very self-image becomes a cliché or stereotype.*

UTA HAGEN

How to Use Acting Methods to Transform Your Image

At a buzzing Hollywood party, Renée Zellweger stands on the table in front of film industry players and sings her heart out. Why? The story goes that she knew *Chicago* was being cast and she wanted to show them what she could do. She knew that unless she showed them that she had it in her to play musical theatre, she'd never be considered. She'd had enough of being typecast, and she was brave enough to do something about it.

'Types' exist in the real world, too. The skills and behaviours you need as a primary school teacher are different from those you need as a City trader, and those demands create industry 'types'. The question is, do you obey the stereotype, confirming how others want to pigeonhole you, or are you brave enough to make some changes, and challenge their view? Recognizable qualities are fine, until they become a straitjacket. Warm and approachable is great – but what if you want to be an MP? It's lovely to be taken seriously for your gravitas and intellect, until you have to host a party and get people dancing.

Cecil Beaton was of the view that breaking beyond your boundaries was the only way. His advice? 'Be daring, be different, be impractical, be anything that will assert integrity of purpose and imaginative vision against the play-it-safers, the creatures of the common-place, the slaves of the ordinary.' Look for these extraordinary creatures in life. Vivienne Westwood transcends the shallow fashion stereotype, as does Paul Smith. Jon Snow combines heavyweight broadcaster with warm, witty human being. Bill Clinton does great world statesman with added warmth, humour and a twinkle in the eye. Anita Roddick went beyond the stereotype of the businesswoman. If you can break out of your 'type' and add new elements you make yourself extraordinary. That has to be good.

Be daring, be different, be impractical

Find your neutral

My own self-image, in a given situation, who I think I am, is not always what I really am . . . if I walk down the street and inadvertently catch a glimpse of myself reflected in a store window, I am appalled at what I actually see.

UTA HAGEN

If you want to make changes in how you come across, you must first understand what it is you're communicating. Here, Frances McDormand talks about the power of understanding how we use the body and the voice. She calls it, in acting parlance, 'the instrument'. Whether you are using your 'instrument' to play a character, or to communicate in a board meeting, the more awareness you have of your habits, the better.

Frances McDormand

The occupational hazard of leading a transformational existence is that one feels like no one in between transformations. The blank canvas analogy is hard to apply to your own person when others and yourself expect more from you than, well, nothing. I've put this into much better perspective since meeting our son. I've had to return from work to be the mother he remembered.

I have never 'lost' myself in work, though there are always behavioural traits that rise to the surface and dominate while I'm creating a character. I have many clothes in the closet that attest to the ghosts of characters past. I can also find lingering reminders of characters in the aches and crooked toes of my own body. The last theatre job I did, Odets' *The Country Girl*, left me with one toe on my right foot slightly more cockeyed than before because of the 4-inch period heels that I would not give up because of how good they made my legs appear. My emotional landscape took a thrashing as well from the repeating eight times a week of a particular truth that I share with the character of Georgie.

I've actually spoken to physical therapists about the lingering ailments of actors. It's like a sports injury. There are scars and adhesions from the repetitive physical and mental gymnastics that an actor performs in the run of a play, just as lasting as ones gained from doing stunts in film work. It's something that can be addressed by keeping oneself in a state of readiness physically, but nothing can really prevent the accumulative affect. Anton Grotowski [leading twentieth-century Polish director and acting teacher] spoke of one's body as 'the instrument'. I subscribe to this analogy. Mine is often out of tune and squeaky but I demand a certain amount from it and find, as I get older, that I have to train physically for the strength and stamina to complete acting assignments to my satisfaction. I still cannot perform an unassisted handstand and intend to do so before I die.

In life, even though you don't need to play a character, it's very useful to develop an actor's awareness of your 'instrument'. We're all a bundle of habits and self-image and if you know what you're doing, you can do something to change it, should you wish.

Habits allow us to get through the complexities of life. You couldn't walk if you had to think about each step consciously, it would be completely overwhelming. Your system auto-mates walking, driving, boiling the kettle, until you no longer need to think about them. That's useful until the point that your habits become chains rather than choices. The habit that makes you talk quietly isn't you – it's a habit. And if you wish to seem more confident, you can choose to talk a different way. It might feel strange at first, but changing a habit is like learning to ride a bike, you have to practise the new habit to make it yours.

Your **self-image** is rooted in what you believe about yourself. It also has an effect on your habits, because mind and body are so inter-linked. How you see yourself affects how you move, which affects how others perceive you, which affects how you see yourself. It can be a vicious or a virtuous circle. The way you think leads you to behave in a certain way. If you think that you're a shy person, and as a result you keep quiet in meetings, then others start to see you as shy too. Your colleagues may not expect you to speak up. They might stop asking you to present, or to contribute ideas. As they reinforce your self-image, your shy habits become more entrenched. The solution is to recognize your habits and the beliefs you have about yourself, and make the decision to do something differently.

You don't need to go to a drama school to develop your awareness of your 'instrument'. You must simply pay more attention. The short sharp shock approach is to watch and listen to yourself on camera. It's usually a hard but useful wake-up to the discrepancy between your self-image, and how you actually come across. You realize there's a difference. Most people are less than pleasantly surprised by what they see. It's one reason why many film actors won't watch themselves on camera.

The most important discovery for actors at drama school is that there is a layer of 'you' beneath your self-image. Actors call it 'centre'. Barack Obama has found his centre And it allows him to communicate with power and simplicity.

In your own life, you will benefit from finding your centre. The secret is to be as aware of the instrument of your body as you are of your brain. It all goes wrong when you become a talking head, something we all have a tendency to do when we're tired or stressed. Your voice gets thin and stuck in your head. You become more locked into self-image than connected to how you feel. You start to define yourself by beliefs, 'you're shy', you're stupid', 'you can't sing', rather than staying centred in your body and your breath.

When you're centred, you're in your body as much as your head. You flow through situations, at ease, natural, rather than judging yourself. Your voice is relaxed and warm and you find it easy to connect with others.

Want to find centre? Breathe easy. Centre is a lot to do with your diaphragm. If you're not sure where it is, laugh out loud. The feeling of really laughing gives you a feel for the diaphragm, your breathing muscle. The diaphragm attaches to your ribs all the way across your torso – think of the skin of a drum. Above your diaphragm is air: your lungs. Below it is your digestive system. Your diaphragm is your centre for your breath, and your voice, responding to and expressing the emotion you are feeling. Breathe as if no one is in the room with you, then you relax. Find that same ease in company and you find 'centre'.

So, tune into your instrument. Start to pay attention to it. Notice how your beliefs about yourself, and your habits affect your behaviour. If you notice that you are getting locked into one gear, take time find your neutral again. Relax, breathe, open up your awareness. Come back to centre. When you move beyond habit and self-image, you can start to grow into the person you want to be, rather than the person you have been.

Change gear

Assume a virtue if you have it not . . .
For use can almost change the stamp of nature
WILLIAM SHAKESPEARE, *HAMLET*, ACT 3, SCENE 3

I remembered reading Aristotle: 'We become just by
performing just actions, temperate by performing
temperate actions, brave by performing brave
actions . . . ' You become what you do.
JANE FONDA

Once you know what your 'neutral' is then it's easier
to change gear. We all adapt our behaviour to different
situations, just as we wear different clothes. Once you have
awareness of what you're doing, you can choose to do something different. If you wish you were more confident, then
you can add in some more confident behaviours. If you feel
that others find you too serious, then you could find a way to
express your lighter side.

Shakespeare's excellent advice to 'assume a virtue if you
have it not' is very useful in life. If you want to be authoritative you must behave as does the authoritative person you
admire. The behaviour triggers the quality in you. It's all

there inside you, every quality you need, but until you change your behaviour you can't activate it.

Aristotle understood the power of habit in transformation: 'We become what we repeatedly do. Excellence then is not an act, but a habit.' What actors learn is that character grows out of behaviour. When *Assume a virtue* you move in new ways, you think in *if you have it not* new ways, too. This wisdom applies to life, particularly in situations where you feel stuck or typecast.

Naomie Harris will tell you what she's learned about extending her range as an actor and will explain how that can help you to access the characteristics that you're looking for in life.

Naomie Harris

I like to be as real as possible and me as me is not a particularly forceful person. I don't want to act anything other than I am – but what acting has taught me is that you have a choice. Who you were yesterday, who you were an hour ago, doesn't have to be the same person that you are now.

Acting allows you to explore the different sides of yourself. In life people get locked into playing one role. You only perceive yourself as your friends and family expect you to be. You only play that particular role. You only discover these other parts of you when something dramatic happens. If the house was on fire, you might discover a courage that you didn't know you had. In acting you discover that you can call on them whenever you like.

The process of acting is amazing. You find that people buy into the act more than the reality generally. If you can act as if you are more confident you will become and feel more confident. The other thing which helps is the way you hold yourself. Play with different positions – hold your head down and clasp your hands in front of you. Suddenly you're vulnerable, you feel afraid. Holding yourself in different postures actually has a mental effect and an emotional effect. You learn so much about the close relationship between the mind and body when you get back in touch with your body. To be strong and confident mentally, it's important to be in touch with your body.

Your voice makes such a difference, too. There are some wonderful exercises that you learn, it's amazing, the different prejudices that brings up in people's minds, not just speaking in the kind of voice that people expect. You don't have to speak in a high voice. You learn that you can choose. A high-pitched voice can

suggest lower status, whereas a lower voice can suggest someone who is intelligent and forceful. You learn that you can play
with the pitch of your voice.

It's really important to realize that you have the potential to
access being any type of person. It's great to know you can pull
that off. If you look at someone who is confident and powerful,
you can take all of that and feed it into yourself to become like
them. You can take those elements of that person and make
them yours.

Naomie has given you some great acting strategies for life.
Just as an actor does, you can bring certain characteristics to
the fore, and store others away. Confidence, energy, calm –
you can begin to assume all of these virtues, and more, if you
go the right way about it.

From an acting perspective you've got two ways of finding these qualities: 'inside-out' or 'outside-in'. The old cliché
is that British actors, with a theatre tradition of voice and
movement training, start with the body (outside-in), and US
actors, with the more cinematic psychological approach of
the 'method', use the mind (inside-out). Because the mind
and body are so interconnected it's more a question of
focus. These days actors use both approaches.

Naomie's suggestion is to focus outside-in. I wholeheartedly agree. It's so much easier to work with the body, than trying to think your way to changes. Stanislavsky agreed, telling his actors that the inside-out approach was much harder to achieve. He said, 'If you . . . begin by thinking about your feelings and trying to squeeze them out of yourself, the result will be distortion and force.'

The outside-in principle works well. Because mind and body are linked, when you move differently, you free your thinking. Harriet Walter explains, 'You alter your posture and that alters your breathing; change your breathing and you can change your emotional state; cock your head on one side and you can change your attitude.'

Think of someone you admire. Focus on their behaviour. What do they do, that you would love to be able to do? Are they super-confident, a devastating flirt, a wonderful host or supremely organized?

Think of someone you admire. Focus on their behaviour

When it comes to taking on a new quality you must observe the detail. Watch a confident person and you will notice that they aren't trying to be confident. Trying to be confident makes you seem nervous. If you want to be confident, the art is to find someone who has the quality you admire, and then focus in on the detail of their dress, their gesture, their posture, their speech and their pace. You learn from taking on one or two details rather than trying to do a generalized 'confident'.

Minnie Driver wanted to overcome shyness as a teenager. Instinctively she began to study confident people. 'It would often manifest as a kind of, gosh, I wish I could do it like that . . . I was bursting with things to say and I had no idea how to say them. They seemed very easy in themselves and their bodies in the way in which they moved through the world. I watched them and I listened.'

You can be certain observation works because you've learned that way before. It's exactly how babies learn. They observe and then copy the behaviours until it triggers the learning within them. If you're brave enough, the best way to find out how someone does what they do is to ask them. Minnie did: 'When I could garner the courage I would talk to them . . . even if you're not there yet you're closer than you were sitting by yourself feeling miserable.' It's always good to chat to people you admire. Find out who inspires them, or how they learned to do it. Often someone's values, or the beliefs they hold about themselves make a big difference. A very confident person might see everyone they meet as a potential friend. That belief could help you, too.

Aristotle said that rather than being about caricature, true imitation gets under the skin, to the 'inner force' which drives the individual to be the way they are. Think about how the person you admire gestures or stands. What do they believe about themselves in order to stand that way, or move that way? Imagine your way into their inner life, and see how that changes how you hold yourself. For instance, you might sense that the person feels safe with others and that belief allows them to stand in a relaxed, open way.

Actors will tell you that often the best way to finding this inner force is through the body, particularly through rhythm. Acting teachers often call this the character's 'metabolism'. Think of the different rhythms of people you know. Simply changing your pace to match theirs is revelatory. Because we each have a distinctive energy it's a good short cut to taking on a role. Find someone's pace, and you unlock their inner life, too. If someone moves with a stately pace through life, try it out one day in a safe space and see what it does for you. Equally, if you want to be perceived as more like leadership material, find a purposeful stride. What actors know is that it changes more than your speed. Fiona Shaw explains, 'Rhythm is the great key to the unconscious. If you pick up someone's rhythm, if you mimic them physically, you get a feel of what they're feeling.'

The imagination is also a hugely powerful tool, and can

inspire you to find a new kind of inner force to meet new challenges. Johnny Depp has said that he uses the instinctive flash of an image in his mind to kick-off his process when it comes to character. For the character of Edward Scissorhands he worked with the images of a baby, a dog and the feeling of unconditional love. Taking an image or a feeling can be a good way to stimulate an imaginative connection to a new characteristic in life.

If you need to lead a group of people, you might imagine the power of a monarch, or a lion. That imaginative shift allows you to subtly embody a different energy. Something new gleams from your eyes, and you notice that people respond to you differently. It's a subtle magic. Sara Kestelman, who has played Gertrude at the National Theatre, and Titania in Peter Brook's legendary *A Midsummer Night's Dream*, suggests that if you need to seem powerful in a board meeting, it may help to think of the colour purple, or to imagine having lots of space around you, even a train behind you. No one else needs to know what you're imagining, but they may sense a shift in your energy. Helen Mirren has said that when she played Queen Elizabeth II she imagined looking down the wrong end of a telescope at the world. That distance gave her the queenliness she needed.

Have fun trying this out. Find someone you admire

who has the quality you'd like. Let's take confidence as an example. Notice what they do that suggests confidence. Notice that it may not be the stereotype. For example many confident people don't stride in, talking in loud voices. The confident person you are observing may be calm, still and quiet. If that's something you admire, try out the detail of the behaviour. Notice how they dress, or stand or gesture. Use your imagination to get a sense of what they think about themselves and others. Intuitively take that on, too. Do any images come to mind that will help you imaginatively? You don't want to borrow wholesale from them, just take a few details and try them out. The art is to be subtle and elegant, making it your version of their quality. Try out one element a day, and see which makes the biggest difference. That's the one to keep.

These apparently simple changes are deceptive. Enjoy making discoveries and then trying them out in a safe space, until you're ready to use them to extend your range in life. When you change your behaviour you trigger profound internal transformation. It gives you a lovely excuse to people-watch, too!

Don't hold back

If you're going to be inhibited in front of everybody and not dare to make a fool of yourself, then you will never get to anything. Unless you can push the boat out, there's no point in calling it back.

JUDI DENCH

The sense of expanding into areas of yourself which have been dormant or repressed is exhilarating, even a little frightening. Do I have this in me?

SIMON CALLOW

If you really want to be yourself but better, then you need to know how to throw off some of your inhibitions. Inhibition comes from the Latin *habere*, to hold. We hold back because we worry that what we have to offer isn't good enough. Theatre director and improvisation expert Clive Barker says it's an insurance policy against failure.

Life is a bit of a risk when it comes down to it, and most people feel scared sometimes. What an actor learns early on in drama school is that until you risk

Until you risk the possibility that you may look foolish, then you get precisely nowhere

the possibility that you may look foolish, then you get precisely nowhere. You learn the most from getting things gloriously wrong, in a safe space. Indeed, getting things right all the time actually prevents you from learning.

Small children are free and confident. They are happy to express their natural instincts and have enormous amounts of creativity as a result. It's only as they grow up that they start to feel shy, ashamed, embarrassed. As an adult if you can re-access a childlike sense of joy in the world, you tap into your creativity, and your full potential. That's why play is so important for actors and children. David Thewlis is going to explain about the power of play, and of trusting your instincts and overcoming inhibition.

David Thewlis

I was raised in Blackpool in a toyshop next to funfair – it's no wonder I've never grown up. As an actor you've got free rein to be quite bold. There's something about acting that's actually quite childish, childlike. It's something we do as children. Children can do it very well. You can have prodigy painters or musicians, or a writer, but they're very rare, but many, many children can act, and act very well.

I don't believe in the word genius being applied to acting. I worked with Marlon Brando years ago, and people said, 'he's a genius, he's a genius', and I said, 'he's not a genius, he's an actor'. He's a very good actor, and he's a very wonderful, brilliant, great man, but he's not a genius. He's not a genius actor, because you can't be a genius actor, it's not really that hard in my opinion. You can be a genius in any other art form, but I don't believe you can be a genius actor. You're really doing lots of stuff you used to do in the playground, running round as Cowboys and Indians, or Doctors and Nurses, or whatever it was you were doing at school, or scoring the World Cup winning goal. I used to love pretending to get shot all the time. I'd drive my mother mad going [machine-gun noise] and falling down the stairs, 'I'm shot!' Like I'm sure lots of kids do, and it's just that I never really got over it. Now I get the opportunity to get shot, and I'm paid for it, or pretending to shoot people. There are times when I do see myself from outside and think, this is just ludicrous, what am I doing, they think I'm this fella and I'm not this fella and everyone's watching me, it just seems very silly sometimes. There's a very childish side to it in a nice way.

You must, as an actor, lose inhibitions, all inhibitions, even if you might flinch sometimes in your private life, your social life.

You will certainly come across points in your career where you must 100 per cent throw all the inhibitions away. You can see when people get nervous they become too aware of everything around them. They're seeing themselves being judged by everyone, they think that everyone's looking at them and judging them in that moment. They get into a panic. I don't know how, or why but somehow in those moments I'm able to go into my peripheral vision and just be in the moment. You have to un-inhibit yourself. If you're shy, go in the middle of the street and shout out, or run around a beach, do something, always try and do something out of character, something new.

You can do far, far more than you imagine you could, it's just fear of the unknown. It's a cliché, but be brave – what doesn't kill you makes you stronger. As long as no one's going to hurt you and you're not going to be judged, the worst you can do is fail, but it's much stronger to try.

Do you remember playing games as a child? Individual egos, inhibitions, doubts and rivalries were left behind and you relaxed into the fun of the moment, playing for the sake of it. You could be yourself, fully, imaginatively, without holding back.

The truth is that anything new contains an element of the fear factor. The source of inhibition is our fear of the unknown and our fear of failure. The very thing we want becomes harder to achieve because we are so frightened of what could go wrong. Observe a person gripped by inhibition and you see someone physically trying to close down. They want to 'curl up and die'. Their toes 'curl' with embarrassment. It may be as subtle as crossed arms or eyes cast down.

If you want to break through your inhibitions, you have to find a way to do something out of 'character', or beyond the persona you've created to survive life. You have to connect to the playfulness that was yours as a child. As we grew up, all of us created a safe, social mask to help us fit in. Essentially, to release inhibition you must re-access a more childlike state. Rather than thinking, 'How am I seen?', which brings on the inhibiting fear of judgement, the actor learns to ask, 'What do I see?', which creates a sense of playfulness and renewed wonder. As adults we would all benefit from taking this journey.

Being able to laugh at yourself is a lovely star quality. It makes people enormously attractive. Compare the easy sparkle of Katharine Hepburn, ready to throw herself into life, with the tight, worried smiles, and even more tightly controlled images of some of the well-known women in the paparazzi age. The most perfectly managed image in the world can't cover up a lack of wit, individuality and spirit.

Shakespeare gives the wisest lines in *King Lear* to the Fool for a good reason; we are all buffoons in our own way, and the best way to find your wisdom, your humility and your humanity, is to embrace that ridiculousness. If you fail to see the funny side you're more likely to be laughed *at*. Ricky

Being able to laugh at yourself is a lovely star quality

Gervais' character, David Brent, in *The Office* is easy to laugh *at*, because he has no sense that he's ridiculous. Don't be a comedy character – laugh at yourself before others do, and find lightness to help you through life. Daniel Day Lewis believes the ability to play is crucial in his work. 'There's always the danger that every step of the way you might simply be a fool . . . That's something you have to learn quicker than anything else – that it's OK to be a complete buffoon.'

Watch the twinkle in the eyes of Nelson Mandela or the Dalai Lama and you will realize that being playful is an extremely grown-up thing to do. The message from acting is that if you want to access your star quality in life, it's all there for you. Break out of your typecasting to take on new roles; extend your range through new pursuits; join a choir; learn to dance; take part in amateur theatre; learn a new sport or craft. Be playful with new possibilities and curious to explore them; discover the lightness and energy that comes from seeing the world with new eyes, and the excitement that comes when others see you in a new way.

Your toolkit

- Understand your image

  What's your self-image? How would you describe yourself? Write down the descriptions you'd use.

  What are your habits? What behaviours do you repeat day in, day out without thinking? What could you do differently? One small change often triggers bigger changes through the system. Walk a new way to work or stand differently and you'll notice changes in other parts of your life.

  Act as if. If you want to add a new quality to your self-image, watch closely those who you admire. Notice what they do differently. Try out one element at a time, without them knowing. Find the one element will make a difference – keep that. Keep adding to your range by observing people.

- **Take on new rhythms.** Put on the TV; find a channel with a presenter; watch them talk and start to mimic their voice tone, pace, body language. Enjoy the way that doing the 'impression' shifts your energy. Change the channel and repeat, with someone else. Be playful, it's a fairly silly thing to do, but when you go back to yourself, you'll find something has shifted.

• **Be playful.** If you want to be able to learn and grow, you have to be able to play and let go of inhibitions. The simplest way to develop a feeling of playfulness in life is to *imagine* the sense memory of having had half a glass of wine. Savouring that lovely melting feeling of all being well with the world relaxes you and helps you to find your lightness again. Actually getting drunk doesn't achieve the same effect, unfortunately!

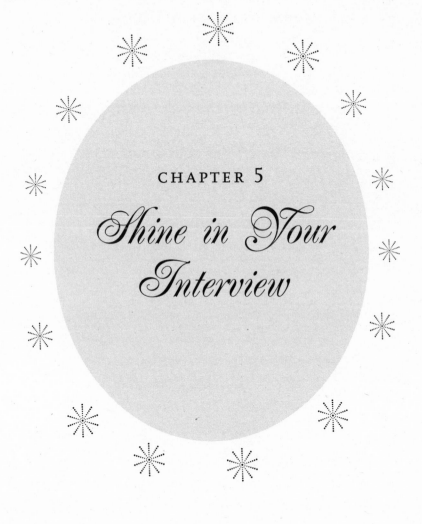

CHAPTER 5

Shine in Your Interview

Remember that in certain situations they're probably going to be as nervous as you. It's a confidence thing. Think, 'they're lucky to have me'. Even when you're younger and desperate for the work, they're still lucky to have you.

ALAN CUMMING

How to Be Yourself and Get the Job

This is it. After endless letter-writing, CV-creating, application-filling and finger-crossing, you've reached the interview of your dreams. Perching nervously in the waiting room, you jump every time a door opens, turning to flash a smile that never reaches your eyes. You attempt to communicate a relaxed demeanour, but it's sabotaged by your heart pounding so hard you fear others can hear it. When you hear your name called, you know that it's now or never.

Interviews are key scenes in the transitions we make in our lives. They are a challenge for any sensible human being because they involve a microscopic level of scrutiny. Every move, laugh and word reveals more about you to your interviewers. They have all the power and the demands of the situation make them necessarily judgemental. This challenging combination can induce extreme self-consciousness unless you have the tools to overcome it.

Fortunately, there is much that you can do to trick yourself out of your anxiety. Once you shift your thinking about the interview, you will relax and let your potential shine through. I'm going to show you how to do that. I will show you how to make a great impression, from your attitude and preparation to your entrance, the show itself and then your exit.

Make no mistake, an interview is pure performance. It is as heightened as theatre, because you have an allotted time in which to shine. Essentially, every move you make matters. If

Interview is pure performance

you are wondering how you can possibly shine under such intolerable pressure, the answer is in your preparation.

You have to plan and rehearse to the point where you can walk in and be like an actor 'in the moment'. It's real; it's natural; but it's carefully edited to highlight the good bits.

Actors are experts at interviews. This may surprise you, but actually, auditions or as they're often called at higher level, 'meetings' are more similar to interviews than you might realise. In both cases you meet your potential employers and you are asked about the job in question and your career to date. In both cases, whether you get the job in a 'meeting' or an interview is often as much about the chemistry and fit between you and your potential employers as it is about your skills and your CV.

Actors are particularly experienced when it comes to making a good impression to employers because *they do many more auditions than most people do interviews,* so they become extremely practised. It's that very perseverance that often makes for success. This chapter will help you to persevere and shine in the interviews *you* face. Good luck!

Success at interview starts in your head

Pessimism is a poison and optimism is a magnet,
and if you can deal with that you manage.

ANNA MASSEY

Believe in yourself absolutely. I don't mean that you have
to be arrogant or think that everything you do is perfect.
Do think that you can do it, that you can succeed, that
you can have a career doing it and that you can be
happy doing it . . . a belief in that is important.

EWAN MCGREGOR

Your success at interview requires that you manifest the belief that you are the right person for the job. Put yourself in your interviewers' shoes. Who would you rather recruit? The candidate who shuffles in, awed and nervous, or the candidate who exudes relaxed confidence, openness and interest? It's an absolute no-brainer.

There's a huge difference between bluff, which is born of insecurity and screams self-doubt, and optimism, which exudes bright confidence and humility. You *don't* need to show off, but you *do* need to show that you deserve to be at interview, and that you are the right person for them.

Sarah Jessica Parker's first lead role was at the age of eight, when she played Annie on Broadway. In the following decades since then, she has experienced many interviews and auditions in her career. Sarah Jessica talks here about the importance of making a small win out of each interview, whatever the outcome, and of building up your confidence and resilience in a situation that can feel out of your control.

Sarah Jessica Parker

Your goal in the beginning should be to feel good that you did it. Find the triumph in that, because that is no small feat. It helps to see the interview process as an experience – hopefully one that is interesting, inspiring, challenging – and to learn what feels good, what doesn't feel good. I believe in that kind of experience. Say to yourself, I just want to know that I did the best I could, this day, this time. I don't need to get the job, that would be wonderful, but just getting through that process is invaluable. The small wins over time add up to something real.

You want to feel good when you walk into the room. Take care about presenting a nice appearance. Feeling attractive, in whatever way works for you, will help you feel confident. And you need to work really, really hard on the interview beforehand. You need to prepare in whatever way is best for you: whether through drawing on your training; sitting in a room by yourself for an hour; or planning for twenty minutes and then putting it away. Feel good about what you can offer. You want to be able to hold yourself together and, more importantly, know what you want to leave that group of people with.

That's why I say, it doesn't matter if you get the job, you just have to feel like: I did it! Go out and run up and down the street and scream and yell. And even if you spend a year doing interviews, you are going to feel really different when that second year starts; you are going to know people, know how you like to work, and be smart enough to know when a job isn't right for you. You're going to be able to ask and answer a lot of questions for yourself. In a business you have no control over, you can control the work ethic that you put in, and know that you did everything yourself.

Optimism and positivity are powerful allies when it comes to interview, fuelling you with the energy to prepare properly and allowing you to communicate the positive gleam of hope. Interviewers aren't psychic and they cannot intuit a positivity about you that you don't already have about yourself. If you can think yourself to a place of quiet calm, dignity and enthusiasm then you have laid the firm foundations of success at interview.

Hope can actually help you to be more successful. Research by C. R. Snyder, Professor of Clinical Psychology at the University of Kansas, showed that hope was the best predictor of good grades in university undergraduates – more so than pure ability. Students with hope motivated themselves to work harder and more creatively to boost their grades.

Ultimately, the reason hope can make you more successful is because it keeps you going. In a study by optimism expert Professor Martin Seligman, optimistic salespeople were found to be more successful – they outsold the pessimists by 21 per cent in the first year and 57 per cent in the second. The optimists didn't let the 'no's get to them. They kept going.

What if you think you're a typically glass half-empty person? Good news! Research showed that although optimism may be partly an inborn temperament, it can be developed. How do you develop it? The art to optimism, Seligman says, is in how you read events. To develop optimism, take these steps:

- **Make universal explanations for success.** Take time to relish the good moments, and let them feed into your sense of self, seeing your strengths as permanent. If the interviewer praises you, take it as validation of your skills and preparation.

- **Make specific explanations for failure.** If you do badly in the interview, don't beat yourself up for being a loser. Ascribe it to a specific reason, in order that you can do better next time, rather than giving up. It didn't work this time. I should have done more preparation yesterday. I wasn't calm enough, I need to relax before.

- **De-catastrophize.** If the interview goes badly, see it as a blip, not the end of your life. You maintain the sense that though life is not all good, it can always get better.

And then, to give your optimism a final polish on the day, you must make sure you walk through that door with the confidence to deliver. You must remember to trust your instinct and to be confident and unafraid; you must walk into the room and think to yourself in a quiet, dignified way, 'They would be lucky to have me.' Then when you walk out of the room, you must remember not to dwell on it. Take confidence in the fact that you've you done your best, and know that it's in the lap of the gods.

Proper preparation

Preparation is important. If you're walking into a
meeting it's good to have got yourself in the frame of
mind for that meeting. Get your mind set.

EWAN MACREGOR

The Royal Air Force maxim, 'Proper Preparation Prevents P***-Poor Performance' is the correct attitude when it comes to shining in your interview. The very fact that you have been invited to interview tells you that your CV has intrigued them. Your challenge during the interview is to confirm the stunning impression that you made on paper. Just as you put effort and thought into your CV, you must put effort and thought into the interview itself.

The purpose of your preparation is to ensure that you are clear about the impression you want to make. Preparation ensures that you are able to relax in the interview. Interview nirvana is achieved when you are able to focus your attention on your interviewers, rather than worrying about everything from the polish on your shoes to the details of your CV.

Here, Bill Nighy talks about the skills he's learned over the years, from both sides of the table, to help you succeed at interview.

Bill Nighy

I find it best to learn whatever it is I have to deliver. Apart from helping me to generally prepare, it prevents me from hiding in any way and it's a sign of respect and seriousness. It also means I don't have to wear my glasses.

It's surprising how many people don't fully prepare. I tried, in the old days, to invent not preparing as a process. It didn't work.

I apparently also had a tendency to look disinterested, if not actually unhappy, in my efforts to appear relaxed. This didn't help, so I learned to lighten my expression.

Allow them to break or fill silences – it's not your responsibility to save the day.

I find I usually regret the third cup of coffee.

Preparing thoroughly for an interview where you're going to be under intense scrutiny is only sensible, and may seem an obvious point. But it's not that simple: not preparing can be dangerously seductive, mainly because not preparing gives you a perfect get-out clause for not succeeding. But, of course, you greatly reduce your chances of getting the job, and the future, you want.

Ewan McGregor knows the cost of not preparing for a meeting. He tells the nerve-racking story of going up, as a young actor, for *Sense and Sensibility*, which Emma Thompson had written and was starring in. He learned the hard way that preparation is crucial. 'It should go down in the shameful annals of history for being the worst prepared meeting ever. And as I was stumbling through, I was thinking to myself, "Just let me go. When I've finished let me go." They were being really polite, and in my head I was thinking, "We all know I haven't done enough work on it." Shameful really. So, I think preparation's really key.'

If the fear of interview makes you go into head-in-the sand mode then the first step of your planning process must be to adjust your thinking from avoidance to activity. One classic actor's trick, which works brilliantly, is simply to remember that there are people on the other side of the table terrified of getting it wrong. Then, you see what you can do to help them. It's devilishly clever because rather than focusing on your neurosis, you focus on others. You give yourself a job to do, one which switches on the real, compassionate human being inside. Your eyes relax and your smile appears, and you suddenly look like a potential employee, rather than the terrified candidate.

'How Can I Help?' is a technique described in neuro-science as 'cognitive reappraisal'. Quite simply, you think about your thinking. If you've spent time turning your inter-viewers into a beast of nightmarish proportions, then realiz-ing that they are actually terrified of getting it wrong makes them seem human again. Suddenly the interview doesn't seem half as daunting any more and you start to feel happier to prepare for it.

Other actors have different ways of reappraising the situ-ation. Gemma Jones uses the frame that she's judging them – rather than the other way round. 'It takes the spotlight off you. Go in and find out do you want to work with them, not do they want to work with you – if *they're* OK. It's not egotis-tical – it makes you more open, you can listen, you're more responsive. It made a big difference, going in with, "Are these people interesting?", as well as "Are they interested in me?"

Both 'How can I help?' and 'Are they *interesting*, as well as *interested*?' are good ways to see a potentially challenging situ-ation in a positive light. Take this curiosity into your research. When your values and passions are the same as the interviewers, an interview becomes a genuinely enjoyable experience. So, find out what you have in common with your interviewers. Apply-ing the three questions an actor uses when they research a character will help you. Google is your greatest ally in this work, but friends and colleagues may well be able to help, too.

- What do the interviewers say about themselves?
- What do they say about others?
- What do other people say about them?

You'll find some interesting and useful ammunition for the interview, but it's not enough. You have to get tough with yourself, and how the interviewers might see you. What doubts might they have about you? How can you allay their fears? Write the questions they might ask you from across the other side of the table. Think through all the information they will want from you, in your words and in your manner.

When you've walked a mile in their shoes, come back to your own. Organize your thinking so that you can present yourself in a way that ticks their boxes. Sociologist Erving Goffman said that the pressure of interview called for what he described as 'dramatization of one's work'. Like a playwright you organize your answers so you can 'dramatically highlight', as Goffman puts it, the elements of you that you want them to see. It's the preparation that goes into the 'natural' performances that you see in TV presenters, newsreaders and radio hosts. A lot of work goes into making it look easy. Even the guests on chat shows have prepared their anecdotes in meetings with researchers.

Alan Cumming explains how it works. 'If you only have to do it for a little bit, it's like taking a deep breath and almost playing a character. It's like when I go on a talk show I feel like I'm playing a version of myself, I don't regurgitate funny anecdotes like that in normal life. I think you can do that for a short burst, you can play a version of yourself that you want to show.' The important distinction is that you are choosing the impression you make, rather than morphing into what you think they want. You must be careful to avoid what Damian Lewis calls 'trying to convey different aspects of yourself, maybe to align yourself a little bit to what you think they're looking for . . . Just be yourself.'

The best way to be yourself is to rehearse beforehand. Practising your answers aloud is gruesome but crucial, because it always comes out differently from how you planned it. When you answer the questions you need to know what impression you want to make on the interviewers. Which criteria are you meeting? What message are you sending out? Be precise about how each answer meets the criteria, and most importantly allows you to be enthusiastic. Don't waffle; find pithy, clear-thinking, enthusiastic answers. It helps to obey the Einstein principle of 'As simple as you can and no simpler'.

Proper preparation can feel less than enjoyable, but it is a huge investment in your future. If you are totally on top of your material, relaxed and yourself, you stand a great chance of making a good impression.

Make sure you shine: Do the work.

Make the right impression

Most people who are nervous want to please. People . . . may be inhibited because they want approval and that can cut off spontaneity.

AL PACINO

They'll probably be on a conveyor belt of people coming in and out and the thing that's difficult with your nerves is that they make you rush into everything. The impressive thing for them to see is that you take your time.

EWAN MCGREGOR

So, the day of the interview has arrived. If you want to make the right impression you must ensure you are as relaxed and at ease as you can possibly be. All the preparation in the world can't take away the adrenalin that hits you when you walk through that door. Drop that coffee, slur your words, laugh inappropriately, and it will be noted.

Like a duck, you may be paddling like hell, but your interviewer needs you to stay composed. Slow and dignified is the answer, as it allows you to resist the siren call of the adrenalin flooding your system, to gabble and rush. You let go of insecurity's bluff, a false con-

Find quiet trust in your abilities

fidence which fools no one. The art is to find quiet trust in your abilities, and ease in your interactions with others.

Emily Mortimer talks here about the importance of letting the interviewers lead, so that you can find ease at interview. When we chatted she'd recently been the one doing the hiring, when she auditioned actors for a play in New York. She'd gleaned insights from the other side of the table that had helped her, and I know will help you, too.

Emily Mortimer

In an interview everything you do is noticed. You are more observed in that moment than you are at most other times in your life. Those first few minutes of a meeting are so important. Get your bearings. You're not just presenting yourself – as in, 'Here I am and you'd better listen'. You need to know what's going to ring their bell particularly. You might think you should 'just be yourself' but there are many different selves and many different ways of being. How one behaves with one's mother is different to how one behaves with one's best friend. That's just how you get on with people.

Out of nerves, some people try to set the tone of the thing. This might feel empowering but I think it sometimes does the opposite. It's like, 'Oh just calm down.' You're pretending to be in a normal situation but you're not in one, so you might as well just behave. The only way to really win is to try to go in with a sort of quiet dignity. Don't barrel in and announce yourself in a loud, show-offy way. Take your time and get a sense of who's there. Let them make the first move. The director Jez Butterworth once told me that the rule for auditions is, 'If there's a piece of paper on the floor, never be the one to pick it up.' Be aware, and wait, and listen.

Separate your preoccupation with your effect on people from what you're actually trying to communicate. It's about concentration, I suppose. Listening is the ultimate tip, and I think it's one of the hardest things to do when you're scared. Let go of worrying about how you're appearing, and concentrate on the conversation that you're having and what it is you're trying to say and what the other person is saying to you. It makes such a difference, and it's just practice and practice and practice. Little tricks to stop you focusing on the fear and to start getting you concentrating on something else.

Ease is impressive at interview, because it signifies self-control in a situation that everyone finds stressful. The art is to appear to be perfectly at home in your dream role.

The 'feeling of ease' is a concept well known to actors thanks to the great actor-director Michael Chekhov (nephew of the playwright Anton Chekhov). Chekhov characterized the feeling of ease as lightness. He talked about the sculpture of Michelangelo and Rodin, saying, 'They are permeated with ease and lightness, which also fills us and makes us lighter.'

Chekhov's advice was that while you must appear to be grounded and strong, you must also find flair and freedom. Physical tension is the enemy. It can make you appear tired and drained, or hyperactive, which bespeaks too much effort.

In order to rid yourself of tension do a physical warm-up beforehand; shake out shoulders, do some yoga. Go for a walk. It's worth it. Ease makes you stand out as charismatic and enthusiastic, in a sea of shaking hands and voices. Notice the times in your life where you are at ease. Then transfer the sense memory of the feeling of ease into more stressful situations.

The waiting room

Be early is the first rule, advises Ewan McGregor. 'If you're walking into a meeting it's good to have got yourself in the frame of mind for that meeting. I'm terrible for getting to places early. I've got it from my mum, she's a real fear of being late, and I very rarely am. It shows you in a really bad light.'

Once you're there, stay hopeful as you sit in the lobby. Kate Winslet warns against letting other people put you off. 'If every other girl is a stone lighter, with longer hair and they're done perfectly, don't doubt yourself, because what they're looking for could be what you are like, not what they are like, because that's the thing that strikes [them] as being more interesting.'

Be dignified. This means being wary of what Anna Massey

calls the problem of, 'So much phoney confidence. You can see it, feel it, it's like a vibration, it's so effortful. You don't have to try too hard. When you are confident, you let people come to you.' While you wait, let yourself 'be breathed'. Let your shoulders relax, sink into the chair and enjoy the fact that because breathing is a reflex, if you breathe out and wait, a breath always comes back. In it comes, there's a pause, and out it goes. It's called tidal breathing because it has the same rhythm as a wave. It's lovely, because when you find ease in your breath, it suffuses your whole system.

In the Interview

When it comes to making your entrance, find the grace that the great art critic John Ruskin described as ease in motion. Take your time as you make introductions. Be alert to the room, so you can adapt your energy to match that of your interviewers. All your antennae are up. Rather than feeling like you have to set the tone, let them dictate the pace and the mood. John Capoccio, the social psycho-physiologist at Ohio University, suggests that the more powerful the person, the more they affect the mood of others. You are the polite, confident guest, they the host. It allows them to play their power and you to seem gracious and at ease.

Be considered. Pauses show that you are comfortable in your knowledge, as long as you appear at ease with them. It is far better to take a couple of seconds to formulate a great answer than to blurt out the first thing that comes into your head. Rufus Sewell has learned the hard way that you can say too much in interview. 'I used to have a tendency to talk myself out of jobs. I'd be so panicked by the pause that I would fill it with whatever came into my head. It took me a while to learn to just sit in silence. They were happy to look at me, I was happy to look back. Don't be afraid of a pause.'

When you really listen it gives you quiet presence

Easy to say, harder to do when the spotlight's on you. How to do it? Rufus advises, 'Just listen, listen out for what's happening, listen out for something to happen. It can feel like an age but it rarely is.' When you really listen it gives you quiet presence and draws others in. It helps to really use your ears, almost as if you are pricking them up as you pay attention to the act of listening. Give your full attention to what is being said.

Listening fully also has a fringe benefit – presence. When you pay full attention to your interviewers you achieve the stillness and focus that signify presence. Mark Strong explains he discovered at drama school that the answer was in, 'Not twitching, fidgeting, moving unnecessarily, just looking somebody in the eye, and being still. I found it through concentration on others. I wasn't watching myself and think-ing, "What do I do with my hands? Should I move?" but con-centrating on what the other people were saying, and doing, and what was happening. That's when people started saying I had presence, but as far as I was concerned, I was just lis-tening.' Trust that when you really listen, you always know what to say next. Don't worry about trying to look clever; pay attention, and, as long as you're prepared, you'll be fine.

And when it's all over and you walk out of the room, feel free to take Sarah Jessica's advice: 'Go out and run up and down the street and scream and yell.' Just make sure you're a couple of streets away before you do it . . .

Your toolkit

- **Think, how can I help?** Plan from the perspective of the interviewers. How can you help them see that you are the right person?
- **Do your rehearsal.** Practise your answers so you can be concise, clear and natural.
- **Get there early.** Sit down, relax and focus. Absorb the mood of the place.
- **Find ease.** You're prepared, so find your poise in the interview. Pause, breathe and take your time. Be dignified.
- **Stay optimistic and enthusiastic.** Believe you can do it – they will see it in your eyes. Show them that you are a positive, passionate person who they will want to take on.
- **Listen.** Aim to listen more than you speak. Imagine you have big bunny ears – it can help you focus your attention on what you're hearing.
- **Be glad you did it.** Once it's over, know you've done the best you can, and chalk it up to experience.

CHAPTER 6

Understanding Others

We can telegraph and telephone and wire pictures across the ocean; we can fly over it. But the human being next to us is still as far away as the stars. The actor takes us on this way.

MAX REINHARDT

With psychology, you practise observing people. You watch people sitting on the subway and you imagine what motivates them, you think about their hopes and their disappointment . . . which is exactly what you have to do when you act . . . To get a real deep, nuanced understanding of human behaviour, art is the best way.

NATALIE PORTMAN

How to Be a Better Colleague, Friend and Lover

Empathy and understanding are at the heart of what it is to be human. All of us can do more to see how others see the world, and to see how others see us.

If you've ever felt that someone else was on a completely different planet from you, this chapter will be of interest. It's about the incredibly different ways we all view the world and each other. It's what makes acting so fascinating and it can help you enormously in life, particularly with the people you find challenging.

When you were little you believed that everyone had the same beliefs and views of the world as you. The idea that other people had whole different universes of experience inside their heads probably came as a revelation. Psychologists call this realization 'theory of mind': around the age of four a child realizes that everyone sees the world completely differently from them. As an adult your ability to connect with others depends on how curious you are to see, and understand their point of view.

In this chapter, I want to help you to deepen your understanding of others, particularly in work and in love. The extent to which you are able to navigate your way through the labyrinth of different perspectives and attitudes which you encounter in life, is largely the extent to which you can enjoy success. Relationships matter, whoever you are and however exalted you become. *All of us need to feel understood* All of us need to feel understood. Taking the time to understand others is spectacularly life-enhancing. I believe it to be the most important star quality of all.

Theatre has a unique toolkit to help you develop empathy. An actor's job is to be professionally curious about the diverse ways in which others think. When an actor looks at a scene, they know that they have the wherewithal to understand and play any of the parts. They know that there are *at least* as many ways to view the scene as there are characters in it.

It's vital to apply this practice to life, too. The more perplexing and impossible the relationship, the more understanding and empathy matter. When you grasp the autonomy you have to improve the quality of your relationships, you'll realize that taking the time to understand others will make you a better friend, a better colleague, and can even help you on a first date.

Change your perspective

There's something endlessly fascinating about different people's points of view and what drives them, what their life stories and situations are. What's great about acting is not only do you go on a journey with them psychologically, but a lot of times physically, too.

CHIWETEL EJIOFOR

You listen, you watch. You try to put yourself in the other person's place: what does she want from you? What do you want from her? You try to be aware of other people's needs. It's very compassion based. Because everyone has needs.

KATHLEEN TURNER

A change, they say, is as good as a rest. Why? Because it's a shift in perspective. Travel is one way to open the mind, but there's a lot of travel that can be done inside your own head, too.

It was F. Scott Fitzgerald who said that the test of a first-rate intelligence was the ability to hold two opposed ideas in the mind and still retain the ability to function. When you challenge yourself to understand the perspectives of others you become more creative and flexible in your thinking.

There's real insight to be gleaned from imagining what the world looks like from someone else's perspective. When you take the time to see someone else's point of view, you build empathy and influence, and over time, trust. When you have trust, anything is possible.

Actors are expert at shifting perspective because it's a professional necessity. They have to find ways to inhabit the views of characters who, in life, they may not agree with.

To help you keep your mind alert to new ways of thinking, Gael Garcia Bernal will talk about the power of multiple perspectives, and then I'll show you how you can apply this sense of wonder to your own life.

Gael Garcia Bernal

Acting allows you to play with this Other with a capital O. This Other that exists in you, you have to play with it, to get in touch with it. You have to understand that Other when you're doing a character and you have to empathize with their emotional journey. It has a big effect, it opens you; it's a way of understanding and getting to understand yourself and other people, and maybe even human nature in general.

Acting is a great way of trying to see things from many sides. The world is what it is, but you can see it in so many different ways. What acting does is say, hey, step a little bit to the right. See how the world looks from this perspective. It helps in life, too, to discover the new angle, express different viewpoints. You discover that it is possible for you to see things differently. You learn the skills to explain a new narrative.

As an actor, you then have to interpret that new viewpoint physically. It has made me, I'm not sure if a better person is the word, but definitely different. You learn that always assuming you are in the right is dangerous.

'Seeing' what someone else sees is an imaginative leap of faith. It's the same skill you use when you read fiction, and it's the reason why fiction has been shown to build the empathy muscle in readers. When you read a novel you must create a mental picture of the characters and locations. When the book is written from the perspective of a first-person narrator you are effectively looking out of someone else's eyes.

Acting is similar. Sara Kestelman explains how it has worked for her in a long and distinguished career.

Sara Kestelman

When you read a novel, sometimes suddenly you're reading something that's absolutely of your own experience. There's a great comfort often in recognizing yourself in whatever is being described. It's those parallel echoes that one finds in characters sometimes. You've had the experience of observing something that has personal echoes, you then delve deeper into your own personal experience, in order to substantiate that. In the inhabiting of the role, there may be a whole learning process about where you are with your own personality in those given circumstances. It might help with insight about how you could do something differently in the future or how you might have dealt with the past differently.

Empathy is all about the journey to another person's experience. When you are curious about the perspectives of others, the world is infinitely fascinating. Everyone you meet can teach you a whole new angle on life.

Listening is the crucial component of the empathy muscle. Partly because so few people do it properly. Ernest Hemingway put it well, 'When people talk, listen completely. Don't be thinking what you're going to say. Most people never listen. Nor do they observe.'

Great actors are, above all, great listeners and Paul Newman had a phrase for bad acting, which applies to life. He criticized it as the 'transmit-*interrupt*-transmit' kind of dialogue, where everyone speaks, but no one listens. Newman admired those who had the mental discipline to *really* pay attention, describing it as the 'transmit-*receive*-transmit' conversation. When you do this you will build bridges rather than walls between people.

A simple way to help you *really* listen is to rest the tip of your tongue at the base of your mouth when someone else is talking. Strange though it may seem, when you talk to yourself in your head, the tongue makes tiny, imperceptible 'talking' movements. Resting the tongue at the base of the mouth, as if you have said all you ever need to say, helps you quieten your internal chatter. Then you are able to fully listen to others and enjoy taking on their completely new perspective on the world. You'll marvel at what you discover.

Take responsibility

*In almost all relationships, or at least in certain areas of
a relationship . . . one person leads and the other follows.
Start with this. Ask yourself how you stand in relation to
the other characters. Are you willingly or unwillingly
leading or following? . . . Is the relationship declared and
open, or is it hidden and subconscious? Is it a relationship of pretended closeness and secret distrust? And
always ask if it is reciprocal or if you are at opposites.*

UTA HAGEN

*Most of the time we prejudge a situation. Acting
taught me what an amazing effect being totally open
can have. Seeing and responding to what is happening
makes such a difference. It's a wonderful lesson, the
effect that really listening can have on someone.
It's a really important skill. All of us need that.*

NAOMIE HARRIS

Jean-Paul Sartre wrote that hell is other people. It's frequently
the case. But it's not fair to lay the blame on everyone else. If
you would prefer to be among heavenly people then it's up
to you to help them find their kinder side. When you take a

different tack with a 'difficult' person, they will, as if by magic, adjust their own behaviour.

When you feel threatened by someone it's easy to create a 'character' for them. They become a stereotyped baddie and you absolve yourself of responsibility. Psychologists call this 'confirmation bias' because it leads you to ignore their good qualities and see only the facets of character that prove your point. You miss the shyness that causes them to seem cold, or the self-doubt that makes them brag. When you choose to see someone differently, you give them the possibility to *be* different.

Here, Imelda Staunton will explain what she's learned about taking responsibility for times of conflict.

Imelda Staunton

Empathy is important. Your job is to be part of the jigsaw, to appreciate what everyone else is doing and to understand their point of view.

I was in a play many years ago, where I could tell the lead actor thought I was a waste of space. He was just waiting for me to finish my lines so he could say his. It was really difficult. I thought, how am I going to sort this out? I decided to ask him for help. I went over to him and said, 'I really don't know how to do this, can you help me?' He really, really, really did. It worked well – it was fantastic. How did I find the courage to do it? It was pride in my work. I wanted to do a good job.

And if there's something wrong then you've got to talk to someone to get it sorted. You can't just sit on it. You need to express it. Don't be afraid to be vulnerable. Don't be afraid to admit, 'I don't know what to do,' or to tell someone, 'I don't know how to do this.' It's good to say I don't know how to do it. If you want to do a good job, you'll find a way.

If you've been in a situation where you've lost your temper, don't go beating yourself up. Look at the situation clearly and try to apply what you have learned. You might think, 'I mustn't do it again, what do I do to avoid it? Next time I'll count to ten. I'll walk away.'

Taking responsibility in moments of conflict is a true star quality. Don't make the mistake of entering a 'victim' mind-set. Blame is easy to dole out but as soon as you think dark thoughts about someone else, you can guarantee that's exactly what they're thinking about you. Glimpsing the physical evidence of your closed mind, they judge you right back.

Take a moment to step back and see the bigger picture, as if you were a director watching from the back of a theatre. Consider the person in front of you with an actor's curiosity, without judgement. Ask yourself what really lies behind their behaviour. People usually have a very good reason – from their perspective at least – for being difficult. Take a moment to see the world from their eyes and work out the best route to bridging the gap between you.

When you see how you might appear to someone else, you are able to find a new approach for them. Imelda didn't blame the other actor, or shirk her responsibility for improving their relationship. She put herself in his shoes and intuited that the best way forward was to ask for help. In fact, Imelda was instinctively doing some disclosure, and working towards a common goal,

Taking responsibility in moments of conflict is a true star quality

both of which are great strategies for trust. However perplexing the situation, if you take the journey into someone else's world you will always find a way out of the maze. Sometimes it won't work. But I'm a believer in trying to see the good in someone.

Update your status

The strongest ones don't raise their voices very much.

MERYL STREEP

*John Wayne told me, 'Talk low, talk slow
and don't say too much.'*

MICHAEL CAINE

Feeling pushed around, ignored and interrupted is horrible. The most common lament I hear from clients is their frustration when they pipe up in a meeting and are ignored. Then five minutes later someone else suggests the same idea and it's received with reverence.

If you'd like to be taken more seriously by those around you, then you'll benefit from developing what the Greeks called your 'ethos': your credibility, your integrity – the trust you inspire in others.

The Romans used the word 'gravitas' to describe a person of substance. It's a good word because it shares its root with gravity. When your words have 'weight' people listen to you. Gravitas suggests that you are a person confident enough to be a leader.

One of the ways actors find their inner leader is through a

system called 'status work'. Status in theatre is a very different beast to status in normal life, which can be signified by your job, your education, your friends, your handbag, even your mobile phone.

Status in theatre is almost animal, in the sense of 'pecking order' or 'top dog'. It's what you assess when you step into a train carriage, or pass in the street. Is the person a threat? Who is going to lead, and who follow? Do you need to move away, or step aside? Status in theatre is physical and vocal, and it's enormously fluid. Your status plummets when you trip in the street. It's why the banana skin is such a comedy classic.

How can you tell if someone has high status? It's largely about ease. Watch a pack of wolves and you can tell which is the pack leader. The lead wolf claims his space with absolute assurance. When he moves, the pack moves. He sprawls, while the lesser wolves defer to him.

At a rock concert at its most electric, you see this extreme status in action. When the rock star glances one way, a whole stadium follows. When they move a hand, the movement sends a ripple through the crowd. This is the highest level of status and it's rare to see it in life, with the exception of military dictators and great political speakers.

That's why in most situations, exaggerated high status doesn't work – unless you want to get into a fight. Keith

Johnstone is the world expert on improvisation for actors, and the originator of status work in improvised theatre. His succinct definition of high status is, 'Keep away, I bite', and he says that low status communicates, 'Keep away, I'm not worth biting.' He knows how much an understanding of status can help in life. An actor friend of Keith's became fascinated by status transactions, discovering that he could use them to help him in Hollywood. Keith explains, 'He played high to agents and directors (and they hated him); he played low and they loved him (but they didn't give him work); he matched status and they gave him leads in movies. "Keith," he said, "they thought I was one of them."' And, as Keith points out, now he is.

Find the right level of status for the situations you find yourself in, and you get the results that you want. When you are conscious of the power dynamics that flow through all your interactions, you will become more effective in your relationships. You will understand why you communicate brilliantly in certain arenas and fail to make an impact in others. To help you understand how to use status in your life, Mark Strong explains how it works for actors.

Mark Strong

Human beings are incredibly astute. Walking down the street you know immediately regarding the person walking towards you whether you're going to stay looking, or just look at the ground. In the light of that, you have to be very subtle when you're trying to create status.

The main thing about status is that *you* don't play it. Everyone around you plays to your status. The king doesn't play the king. Everyone else plays to the king, so he doesn't have to do anything. That ease is what gives you high status.

Status is about bearing, but you can overdo it. Doing too much of it looks like you're trying too hard and it doesn't work. Watch *The Apprentice* and you see those people puffing their chests out and talking themselves up. You don't believe a word. They look ridiculous, they are taking the trappings of what they think is required. It's so obvious it's not working.

More than anything I think you have to learn how to believe in yourself. You have to trust, to tell yourself, that you are as good as the next man or woman. You have to imagine yourself at the centre of everything. In your mind you are thinking that what you have to give is important.

There are two examples of how you can raise your status. One is by going against the perceived way you're supposed to behave, because you're so casual with the way you're supposed to behave that you're able to do the complete opposite. You send the message that you're so at ease you're able to do the exact opposite of what others expect. The other way is to draw everyone into you. A schoolteacher once said to me that if I ever found myself in a situation where people were having a conversation that was going way over my head, the best thing to do was nothing. Not to say something out of shame at not taking part in the discussion. Not to say something to attempt to display my intelligence and compete, but just to listen and observe. Not only might I learn something, but his theory was that after a while everyone else would wonder what I was thinking and their own insecurities (which we all have in one way or another) might lead them to wonder if I wasn't actually the smartest person in the room.

I'm like that in life actually. If I'm in a group of people, and somebody's talking, I just look at them and listen. I don't start moving around. Concentrating on what's going on around you allows you to be still, because then you're focusing on that rather than yourself. Paying attention is at the core of a lot of it, it's about not looking at yourself. It's what I think acting is all about. It's all about losing your self-consciousness.

Status cannot be demanded. It can only be earned. The trick is to know how to create the ease and stillness that draws everyone in. Trying too hard to force your power on others reveals to them that deep down, you're scared. Shouting and showing off are all status killers. Teenagers innately know this. They are the masters of status because they are focused on its evolutionary purpose – finding a mate. Any teen will remind you that if you want to pull, you have to play it very, very cool indeed.

It's not all about high status. I always encourage clients to develop their natural warmth at the same time as their gravitas. Star quality is about finding the perfect combination, then adapting to the situation you're in. Sometimes you're required to lead, and sometimes you aren't. Imagine hosting a party as if you were the chair of a board meeting. Everyone would be too terrified to talk. Imagine chairing a board meeting as if you were the approachable host of a convivial party. No one would take you seriously.

Of course, you can only earn status if you have the substance to support the style. Your behaviour, experience and values must first be worthy of the respect of others. You need to have developed your

Shouting and showing off are all status killers

knowledge and expertise to the extent that when you lead, you have something to say. You have to have done your apprenticeship, and then when you have the skills, you're ready to take the stage.

If you are to convince others to follow you, you must emanate the stillness that encourages them to believe in you. We all follow before we lead, learning the low-status behaviour that makes us approachable and employable. When invited to play a leading role, whether in a presentation, as a tour guide, or as a parent, you must own the mantle of leadership. A leader who seems to doubt themselves is unnerving for those who follow them.

Actors usually play a certain kind of status, as much due to casting directors as to their personal choice. Clint Eastwood, Angelina Jolie and Helen Mirren are good examples of actors who play 'high status'. Woody Allen and Renée Zellweger play great low status. In life, most of us have a preference, although it does depend on the context.

The first question to ask yourself is where you are on the high–low status continuum. Are you the gravitas type? Or are you warm and approachable? Are you happiest leading or following?

You will know if you're a high-status player, because you always, always get served at the bar. When you speak, people listen. When you are silent, people take note. You ooze authority from every pore, but you may be accused of being cold and unapproachable.

If you tend to be more of a low-status player, you are happier to focus on others. People will see you as approachable, warm and you are easy company and a congenial host. However, they may say that you lack gravitas, or that you are a pushover, a people-pleaser. Most people are a complicated mixture of the two.

Mark has given you a great guide to playing a relaxed, easy high status. Neither too low, nor too high. He's right. My feeling is that somewhere in the middle is a good default position. You can do gravitas when you need it, and you're able to light up the room with a warm smile, too. This ability to adjust gravitas and warmth, depending on the situation, is an elegant star quality.

So, what are the rules for playing gravitas when you have to lead?

- **Own the space you're in.** Jane Fonda has observed that women often find this a particular challenge. 'I continue to be amazed by the number of women I consider strong leaders, who still worry about "taking up too much space in meetings".' To own space, use your voice to fill the room. Voice is made of vibrating air molecules, and you need to send them right across the room if you are to have gravitas. Even if you are talking quietly, you must have a sense of sending your voice to the furthest wall.

If you want to be able to do this then a simple warm-up before you get there is to yawn and speak, or sing, to free the voice up. When you sing you send the sound further and with more energy. You also need to do what Keith Johnstone calls letting your 'space flow into others'. It demands open body language. Uncross your arms, unbow your head, stop touching your face and you open yourself up to the room, raising your status instantly.

- **Keep your head still.** It has the biggest effect of all. It's well worth getting it right, and you may need to practise in a mirror. Make sure you don't nod, and don't raise your eyebrows when you speak. You instantly feel more powerful. It can help to imagine a book is balanced on your head, so you can't do lots of nodding. This stillness of the head can be a powerful trigger for other high-status behaviour, so if you do one thing, do this.

- **Hold eye contact.** The more powerful the person, the more confident they are to stare other people out. If you're tense it can look extremely aggressive, so be careful to stay relaxed and friendly with it. Keep your eyes soft and relaxed. Three seconds is enough to let your eyes glue onto someone for a moment. I've heard it described as 'sticky eyes'. It's extremely flattering, and high status when you get it right. If you want to lower your status, glance away.

- **Relax and align your posture.** Imagine how tall and grounded you would feel if you were standing in a great open space, with no one else around. You want that easy alignment, the long spine and the sense of your feet planted on the ground.

- **Take John Wayne's advice:** 'talk low', try gesturing with palms down, as opposed to palms up. Palms down gestures have an instant effect on your vocal tone, making it lower and more authoritative. Switch to palms up and you notice that your voice becomes more musical and approachable. You have the choice!

- **Talk slowly.** Less is more when it comes to status, so slow down and make your words count. You also have to be happy to hold a pause. Saying 'um' is very low status, because people use it to fill pauses. If you want gravitas – don't. Be happy with a pause, it raises your status enormously.

Play with these techniques and find those that work best for you. Then try them out with strangers. If you are playing a level of status that is unhabitual then it may feel very unusual at first. It's best to practise it with people who don't know you until it becomes more comfortable. Supermarkets, airports and stations are wonderful places to practise status. If you get it right at the airport you may even get upgraded . . .

Be warned: without the balance of warmth and gravitas you become cold and authoritarian. You may only need the stillness of high status 5 per cent of the time. It's a matter of understanding your habitual level of status, and the demands of the roles you play, then finding the right balance. If you lead, you may need to play high status at work, but make sure you lower your status when you go home. Play between the gears so you have both the gravitas *and* the warmth that you need at your fingertips.

Curb neediness

There's a great line in Broadcast News *where Albert Brooks says, 'If only needy were a turn-on.' It's hard, going after what you want without seeming needy. It's one of the great tragedies of life that being needy is such a turn-off. All you can do is try to find ways of pretending that you're not.*

EMILY MORTIMER

150

> *There's a level of you that has to be OK no*
> *matter how things turn out, because the*
> *universe doesn't work with desperation.*

OPRAH WINFREY

Have you ever noticed that when you fall in love, suddenly a number of potential suitors appear? But that when you are single and lonely you find yourself in a love desert? There's a very good reason. It's because neediness pushes others away from you.

This catch-22 causes so many of us to sabotage our heart's desire, in work and in our personal lives. In the complicated dance that is human relationships one of the biggest lessons of all is that the more you desire something, the less you must signal it to the object of your affections.

There are lots of rule books that tell you how to play the game so that you can make the object of your affection fall for you. The trouble is that they make you manipulative. It doesn't work, because we all know when we're being manipulated and it's not attractive. The antidote to neediness is simple, healthy self-respect and a big dose of chutzpah. It's a trick you must play on your mind.

To assist you in this quest, Frances McDormand will tell you about the time she behaved with self-respect, chutzpah and integrity in a very early audition and came away with a job *and* a husband.

Frances McDormand

I learned this from my husband and collaborator Joel Coen actually. I've benefited from his view from the other side of the table. That table being the audition/interview table and his position being the employer and I the employed. We met at my audition for his first film *Blood Simple*. It was a very early audition for me and I had not had many for film. I had only been given two scenes from the screenplay to prepare. After reading them and chatting, Joel and Ethan asked me to come back that afternoon at 2 p.m. to read with one of the other actors that had already been cast. I said no, I couldn't come back at 2 p.m. because my boyfriend had a one-day role on a soap opera and it was showing that day and I wanted to watch it.

They have subsequently told me that by saying that, I probably got the job. The chutzpah of it, I guess. They asked if I could come back *after* the soap opera had aired and I said yes. So they gave me the script, I read it and came back at 4 p.m. to read. I was cast as Abby in *Blood Simple*. It was my second job out of drama school and my first movie. I have been in six of the Coen Brotherhood's films and have been in a relationship with Joel Coen for twenty-five years.

I have learned that no matter how much fame and fortune you may gain, saying no is still the most power one can wield. To keep control of my life, I have made the decision to say no to doing press and publicity for the past five years. I found that I was having to answer to celebrity rather than to my work and it was very distressing. I have managed to get work because of my work and not because of whether or not my picture is in the latest fashion magazine articles.

I must take the risk that I will not always get the work I'd like and may have to accept less money if my employers feel cheated of the publicity element of an actor's contract. But I feel much more in control of my personal life. If I don't exploit myself publicly and only concentrate on exposing myself as a character in a play or film then I feel my decision is justified. This is, of course, not an easy position for a young person beginning their career. I only offer it as a suggestion as how to manage one's life.

When you sparkle with life and chutzpah, you make an impression. And when you communicate self-respect and integrity, that's a dazzlingly attractive combination.

Neediness kills this *joie de vivre*. When you go into a situation and behave with neediness you are communicating what psychotherapist Thomas Harris called, 'I'm not OK, you're OK.' You become like a child looking up at the grown-up on a pedestal. It's desperately unattractive to the other person because they wonder why you need them so much. It suggests that you don't have enough in your life. Frances' story shows that it's not about pretending not to be needy, it's about genuinely having other places and people that matter to you. Game playing never works, because it comes out of 'I'm not OK, you're OK' thinking.

When you want to spark up rapport you have to get into 'I'm OK, you're OK' thinking. When you go in as an equal, with your individuality and your self-respect intact, then you don't become dependent or clingy. See the human being in front of you and relate to *them*, rather than an exalted idea of their greatness. The more comfortable you can be in yourself, and the more natural you are in your relationship with them, the more chutzpah and integrity you will manifest.

The 'I'm OK, you're OK' principle is an absolute must-have on a first date. That doesn't mean placing complete trust in a stranger, but it does mean that you keep an open mind.

Be mindful of the two main ways that nerves – and need – can sabotage you. Some people get all haughty and defensive, 'I'm OK, you're not OK.' It's often that you don't want to seem needy, but if you go overboard you will keep everyone, however nice, at arm's length. Don't be too quick to judge, even if they don't meet all your criteria. Treat them as a potential friend, let them relax and then you can both work out if you enjoy each other's company. Giving them the benefit of the doubt (as long, of course, as you're in a public place, and people know where you are) allows for the potential of a spark. They may not seem like The One when they walk into the room, but The One may not come in the form you expect. Don't close your mind too early.

Use your empathy skills to help. Nerves make people do all sorts of strange things, such as bragging about their lives, or seeming ill at ease. Rather than letting this affect you, see the desire for approval that usually underpins all the strange behaviour. Let them see that you accept who they are, even if it's only for a few hours. Then they relax, and you'll get a sense of the real individual underneath all the effort. If you like the person beneath the nerves, you'll want to meet again; if not, say goodbye politely and move on.

If you do get on really well, stay in 'I'm OK, you're OK' once the date is over. That means you get on with your life and if they call, they call. If they want to see you again, great, but remember, 'They're OK, you're OK.' You have a full life already, and they will have to fit into that. Don't make the fatal mistake of dropping the rest of your life at the first sign of interest. The more 'I'm OK' you are as a person, and the richer your life is, the more others will relax in your company, and the more you'll have to offer them.

Put simply, when you become playful and positive about life, you are able to give attention to others. It's so much more life-affirming than the desperation of 'I'm not OK, you're OK,' which drags others down. Give others the gift of appreciation and admiration, the experience of how it feels to be seen, admired and desired.

When you become playful and positive about life, you are able to give attention to others

When all is said and done the art of relationships is all about the perspective that comes of understanding others. When you are able to move beyond your own obsessions you become a great human being. You see the bigger picture, and you contribute to something more important than yourself.

Your toolkit

• **See the other side of the story.** There's always another way to look at the situation, however perplexing it may seem. If you're really stuck when it comes to understanding someone else, try this. Lay out three chairs. The first chair is your perspective. Sit in that chair and write down what you think about the situation, and about the other person. Move to the second chair. This is the other person's perspective. Write down what they think about the situation, and about you. Now move to the third chair. See the two of you interacting, as if from a distance. What advice would you give you?

- **Update your status.** People relax around others they perceive to be similar to them. If you want to build a relationship with someone, and it seems like they are on a different planet, maybe you are playing the wrong status. Ask yourself, do I need to follow, or lead in this situation? If you need to lead, play high status, or gravitas. If you need to follow, play low status, or warmth.

- **Place your voice.**

  For **gravitas**, try (before you leave the house) tapping your tummy, as you say the days of the week, or jog on the spot. The voice comes out with a low tone that is easy and relaxed. It's extremely credible sounding. The simplest way to hook into it is to gesture with palms down.

  For **warmth**, tap your chest, imagine someone you love, and say the days of the week to them. Send the sound through your chest. This has a much warmer, richer sound, it's great for approachability. Gesture with palms up to find it quickly. Speak from the heart. Nod your head a lot, raise your eyebrows, smile. Touch your face and relax your posture. Close your body language so you don't fill the space so much.

- **Find common goals.** The quickest way to build trust is to find common goals. If someone feels that you have taken time to understand their perspective, and to work with them to a goal, they will begin to trust you.

- **Draw others in to you.** Rupert Everett's secret, which is great for a date if you want to get the other person to lean in, is to speak softly. He explains, 'Always speak as quietly as possible. It draws the listener in and makes you look riveting as well as beautiful.' Make sure they can hear you though!

CHAPTER 7

*Enjoy Your
Big Speech*

I used to get very nervous about public speaking. I'd feel ill, my hands would shake, the whole thing. I found my own way to do it. It's important not to act it – you have to be yourself – and it's important not to pretend.

DAME HELEN MIRREN

I think it's also about trust . . . Trust that who you are and what you're doing is more than enough. Don't be desperate; don't be aggrandizing; don't try and gild the lily. Do what you've got to do fully and completely, and then it's done. And you will be in service to something else.

LAURA LINNEY

How to Overcome Your Nerves and Make Your speech with Confidence

'We'd love it if you'd do a short speech.' These words have the power to drive terror into the most stalwart of hearts. Most US citizens say they are more terrified of public speaking than of death. One in five people claim to suffer from the fear of public speaking, glossophobia, which translates as 'fear of the tongue'. It's similar to claustrophobia because it causes sufferers to feel trapped and panicky in front of an audience.

If you've been asked to speak and are feeling apprehensive, relax. In this chapter I will show you that you can *enjoy* giving your speech. You can move from the belief that speeches are terrifying, to the belief that speeches are a good challenge, and a *great* adrenalin rush. You may even learn to enjoy them.

Public speaking is a skill that is well worth acquiring. When you become known as a confident, accomplished speaker you will find that all manner of doors open. Good orators get the best jobs, because they look and sound like leaders, and they are happy to be visible. There are so few good speakers out there that even if you do a half-decent job, you'll stand out. It's well worth making the effort, because in the end, star quality is all about taking on the challenges that others are scared to.

If you feel frightened, you're in illustrious company. Actors all feel fear. Dame Eileen Atkins explains, 'We're all terrified all the time. The

Star quality is all about taking on the challenges that others are scared to

only thing to do with fear is to *use* it.' An actor would worry if they *didn't* feel fear before a show. Nerves ensure that you put the work in, and they focus your mind and body on the task. It's only when your nerves get out of hand that they damage your performance.

So, what's the secret to enjoying your speech and impressing your audience? It's simple. You must plan thoroughly and thoughtfully with the audience's needs in mind. You must get mind and body into a focused, relaxed state before the speech. You must control your nerves. Then, in performance you must be enthusiastic, clear-thinking and focused on the audience.

Embrace the risk

*It's a question of am I going to be the little kid, to
run and hide behind mummy – or am I going to be
a grown-up and pull myself together and be courageous?
If you take a risk then life becomes very rewarding.
It's scary at the time . . . but boy the adrenalin
rush is worth it afterwards.*

SOPHIA MYLES

*As far as being afraid, I'm always afraid . . . if I'm not,
there's no point doing it. I'm always like, can I do it?
What do I need to know? What can I learn?*

FOREST WHITAKER

Making a speech is always a risk. With a live audience you never quite know what will happen, and it takes trust and confidence to deal with the uncertainty. That's exactly what makes a good speaker so impressive. They embrace the risk and rise to the challenge.

Life is full of risks. Every time you fly in a plane you take a risk. You know this as you embark, but you take confidence in the calm demeanour of the pilot. Their voice tone as they introduce themselves on the intercom tells you that they

163

are credible and calm, ready to deal with anything that occurs. If they sounded nervous, you would quickly lose your composure. You need your pilot to seem calm and in control, whatever happens during the flight.

When you make a speech you are the pilot of the plane. Your audience needs you to show them that, whatever happens, they are in safe hands. There is nothing worse than a speaker who is shaken by something that goes wrong. Their voice starts to quake, and their confidence slips away. Imagine hearing that fear in-flight in the voice of your pilot. You'd be terrified. Your audience will feel the same if you are thrown by events.

What's the solution? You must learn to embrace the risk of performance as part of the fun. You must learn to welcome a little bit of turbulence: the late-comer, the difficult question, the IT failure, *and to know that you will cope*. Pilots learn in flight school to deal with all manner of eventualities. A confident speaker takes the same attitude. You are aware that in live performance events may not happen as you expect them to, and you have the relaxed confidence to know you are prepared enough to cope if they do.

To help you with your speech, Ewan McGregor talks here about embracing the risk of live performance, and learning to enjoy it.

Ewan McGregor

With performance there is no get-out clause. You can't go on and say, 'Ladies and Gentlemen, I can't do this, sorry.' You couldn't allow that to happen. I saw a singer in America who'd agreed to sing the national anthem at the Super Bowl. She was terrified. She walked out there, and the camera followed her. If on the day someone had said, 'Will you do this?' her fear might have stopped her. She managed to do it, because she'd agreed. When you've already said you'll do it, you have to. Even when you say yes, you know you will be scared, but you think how great you'll feel afterwards, how great it will be to do it.

There's also a kind of acceptance of the fear. One of the ways you deal with it is by talking about it beforehand. The nearer you get to the performance, the more and more horror stories you tell each other about 'drying' and people that have 'dried' and famous 'dries'. That becomes part of it. It's like facing up to it by talking about it a lot. It's an important part of dispelling it, going OK, it can happen.

And if you're doing a speech and you lose your place, I've learned it's not the end of the world. I dried up in *Guys and Dolls* during a song. At the time, it was a nightmare. I went on and I started singing to Jenna Russell. There was no reason for it, I just looked over and suddenly my mind went blank.

The orchestra can't stop, so I came in behind the music, in front of the music. I started singing, 'I like to look at your face . . . I like it a lot'. Finally the conductor belted out the end of the song. We both heard him and we came in and finished it, but it was awful. I went into my dressing room and I was completely grey, like I'd been in an accident. All the blood had left my face. I tried everything to persuade myself it hadn't happened, but it had. It was horrible.

A week afterwards I was still completely rocked by it. I had a chat with Douglas Hodge about it. He said, 'What you want to know is that it'll never ever happen again, and you can't know that. That's what makes it great, and in the moments where it does go wrong, that's what makes it awful. If you can accept that, then you'll enjoy it. If you want to know that it will always be perfect – you can't.'

He was right. He helped me think OK, nobody died. People still enjoyed the show. He made me realize that the majority of people in the audience, if something were to go wrong, would only want for you to recover and carry on. Most audiences just want to have a nice time. They only want for you to do well. At the end they give you a big clap. It's rare that they're thinking, 'Oh my God, he's terrible, he can't do it.' But you hear all those voices in your head.

I don't think anyone comes to watch you fail. There were even people there who said that they didn't notice. I couldn't believe it, but it's important to remember that if you make a mistake, most people don't notice. You're allowed to get it wrong, it makes you more human.

Going out in front of a West End audience after 'drying' the night before is about as scary as it gets for a performer. The good news for you is that because Ewan had to learn the hard way, his advice for coping with risk is crash-tested for you under extreme conditions.

To enjoy performance you have to embrace risk. The art, like the pilot of a plane, is to stay cool, calm and in control when you hit turbulence. To do this you need to understand what stress does to your body. The panic you feel when faced with the staring eyes of an audience actually happens for an eminently sensible reason. The unpleasant heart-thudding, palm-sweating and voice-trembling is all to do with a physiological process going on under your skin.

Why does it happen? Your primitive ancestors didn't like being stared at. Not one little bit. Staring, especially when it involved a large group of strangers, meant trouble. 'Fight or flight', your early warning system, is triggered. Stress hormones flood through you. Blood supply is diverted to your limbs and heart, and away from the front of your brain. Your body reasons that you need to stay and fight – or run.

This alarming response can feel out of control. Mainly because blood is being diverted away from the reasoning part of your brain. You are unable to think straight when it's happening to you. The feeling of being out of control, and vulnerable can make you think that performance is not for you. If you relive bad experiences, you increase your anxiety. Even when those bad experiences were at primary school. If you're going to be able to feel confident about speaking to an audience, you need to know why the bad memories have such a hold. And then you need to know how to banish them for good.

When you feel humiliated, rejected or laughed at, the brain's fear centre, the amygdala, gets activated. Joseph E. LeDoux, a researcher at New York University, discovered that each time you experience your fear, and the memory that triggered it, you open the 'file' exactly as you last stored it. How you feel about the memory depends on whether you modified it the last time you looked at it. If you haven't changed your perception of the event, LeDoux tells us, the fear deepens. When the memory has a hold over you, just seeing it in your mind's eye can make you relive the anxiety. But, thankfully, your memory and the fear attached to it can be reconditioned, lessening its power over you.

You can do this in two ways. Firstly, you can rethink the actual event and see it in a different perspective. What Ewan did first was to re-evaluate the memory. Douglas Hodge helped him to see that it wasn't that bad. He took the incredible humiliation out of it and gained a new perspective. Secondly, and you must do this, you need to do the very thing you fear. Then your fear lessens and you are able to move on. Ewan got back on stage (admittedly he had little choice).

Do the same; even if things have gone wrong in the past, don't let it stop you now. Have the courage to get back up and give yourself some positive memories to look back on. Take comfort in the fact that most people are so busy worrying about their own failings and inadequacies that yours hardly register.

If you want to make your speech easier choose a small, sympathetic audience, and not Carnegie Hall. Once you've done the speech, pat yourself on the back and then let it go. Knowing that you can deal with whatever happens, gives you a deep-seated confidence in yourself. You even discover that, when you embrace the risk, you become an excellent speaker, because rather than trying to control everything, you relax into it.

First night nerves

Nerves are inevitable. It is no use hoping to banish them entirely, so the obvious thing is to utilize them. To do this successfully requires humour, technique and strong will.

NOEL COWARD

Actors dread first nights. They are said to be as stressful for the body and mind as a car-crash. Though they may appear calm on stage, actors are just as terrified by the prospect of everyone staring at them as you are. The urge to run and hide when the moment of performance approaches is universal.

You may not have theatre critics waiting to appraise your performance, pencils at the ready, there is no doubt that a speech can be terrifying. Fortunately for anyone feeling the dread that accompanies imminent performance, there's a handy psychological toolkit to help.

It's important to learn the toolkit. You mustn't let your nerves get to you. I've known clients lose sleep for days, even weeks, before a speech. It's an awful waste of your life, and it's perfectly possible to manage the fear if you know how.

Here, Bill Nighy talks about facing nerves and self-consciousness to do a great performance.

Bill Nighy

It is perfectly legitimate to be afraid in these circumstances. It's a healthy, normal reaction. You are supposed to be afraid. Only the mad are not.

It seems I can operate successfully, even whilst my head is projecting doom. Which is fortunate.

I sometimes try and consider first night nerves as I would an illness. It is not unlike being ill and I can act when ill, so why not with nerves?

It helps me to think of myself as part of a company who are about to tell a story: my job is to help them to do that.

Don't take drugs. Pay your taxes.

If you want to know how to operate, even as your head is projecting doom, then you need to know how to smite the nasty little gremlin of 'Creeping Dread', or, in psychology parlance,

'Anticipatory Anxiety'. If you invite it in, it creeps into your soul and wraps its icy hands around your heart.

Creeping Dread is about the world you fashion inside your head. When you know how to adjust your inner imaginings you can shift your anxiety into a state of readiness. How you visualize makes a huge difference to how you feel about your speech. Make images in your mind's eye of all the times your speechmaking has gone wrong in the past, and you're guaranteed to get nervous. Creeping Dread's a vampire: when it strikes, you've invited it in by visualizing negative moments. Don't. Do the opposite and banish it with good memories.

Make a mental photograph album of times when you've felt confident and achieved your goal. Then, the next time you feel pangs of anxiety hit you, sit down in a comfortable spot; look up at the sky and take a moment to remind yourself of times that it has worked. See yourself in those moments where you pulled it off, and remember how good it felt. Know that if you could do it then, you can do it now. Use those 'photos' of your successes as evidence. Know that each time Creeping Dread breathes its icy breath into your heart, you can knock it out with a good memory.

You can also adjust how you *talk* to yourself. It's useful to be aware of the two voices in your head, sometimes called 'Self 1' and 'Self 2'. 'Self 1' is the calm and confident you, the one who performs with panache and poise. 'Self 2' is the you that gets het up, anxious and critical. It particularly loves to sabotage you by presenting you with doom scenarios.

The art to great performance (but not necessarily great rehearsal) is to tell Self 2 to shut up. If you have a voice in your head that says, 'But you'll never be able to . . . What if it goes wrong?', and it makes you feel nervous, tell it to shut up and you will instantly feel much more confident.

You don't have to be rude to 'Self 2'. You can address it, with a charming tone, saying 'Thanks so much', before telling it to get out of your cranium. You can argue with it too. If 'Self 2' presents a doom scenario you can replace the bad 'What Ifs?' and 'Buts' with 'What if it goes well?' and 'But you know how to do it.' Talk back to the mean voice and refute its negative predictions, with positive ones. However frightened you are, there's always something you can do to feel better.   You can choose to be bigger than the fear and to get on with what you have to do.

When first night nerves hit, remember that the world inside your head is your domain. You decide how to perceive your experience. If you start to feel anxiety rise, take hold of what you're doing to yourself through the inner movies and soundtracks that you play in your head. Turn the negative scenarios into positive ones, and notice that your emotion changes. Make sure that your mood is productive, because it is crucial that you are feeling positive enough to do the preparation for your speech. If Creeping Dread turns up uninvited, smite it, and get on with what you have to do. You're in charge after all.

If you work hard enough, there is a level beyond which you cannot fall . . . It might be that inspiration doesn't strike, but that could still be enough to have you feeling like you're not on a sinking ship. Know you've done enough to get through this, no matter what happens.

EMILY MORTIMER

If you want to make a brilliant speech, then you must prepare for it. Theatre is military in its discipline because great performance is *always* born of thorough preparation and rehearsal.

The apparent ease of a great speaker is akin to the studied artlessness of the very well dressed. Those who *seem* to ad lib have usually done the most work. Making it look easy is not as easy as it looks.

Knowing your material thoroughly is an absolute essential

If you wish to join the ranks of these poised orators you *must* put in the work. Knowing your material thoroughly is an absolute essential. A great speech is elegant in its simplicity. Comprised of well-crafted ideas, it is spoken clearly and, most importantly, it is spoken from the heart.

Preparing matters for two reasons. Firstly, because you are speaking for the benefit of others, it is your duty to make sure that you have something considered and interesting to say. Secondly, preparation matters because it is the most effective way to calm your nerves. The voice that whispers, 'What if you forget what to say next?' kills your confidence.

So, how do you work on your speech? To start with, you need some words. I asked playwright and scriptwriter Sir David Hare for his advice on crafting language for perform-ance, so that you can focus and distil what you want to say in your own big speech.

David Hare

I'm so hard-line. Your own feelings in terms of your own perform-ance are irrelevant. Nerves are vanity. It's a form of courtesy to be heard, it's just polite. Just as you wouldn't tread on people's toes or you wouldn't give them a glass of ditch-water and call it wine, you don't call them into a room and not have spent time organ-izing your thoughts so that you don't waste their time. If you can think of it as not being about yourself, but about them, it will sort itself out magically.

If you think of it as manners, meaning that you will make everybody else uncomfortable if you don't raise your voice, then it's not about self-projection. It's not about being a boomingly dominant person in a room, it's not about your own feelings, nor about your own identity. It's about how do I make sure that the next fifteen minutes is not miserable for them? If you get up and the first thing you say is 'I'm hopeless at giving speeches', then you have already made your own qualities, rather than your subject matter, the focus of the speech. It's an act of pure self-advertisement, and is unforgivably vain. The temptation is to yell out 'Who cares?' and 'If you don't like it, don't do it.'

You don't have to be the protagonist of the drama. If you think of it all as a psychodrama, 'Will I have the courage? Will I be able to?' then it's the wrong drama. It's not about your success or failure in the room, it's about not being rude. It's good manners to make sure you've got something worth saying.

If you say what you feel, you can't go wrong. Speeches at weddings are almost always wonderful, because they are heart-felt. High-emotion occasions like that, in a way, are easier.

When someone has been in agony about a speech, 'David, you can do this, it's your business, you're a writer' I've just said, 'Stand up and say what you feel, but write it down, for God's sake, so that you know what it is you want to say.'

When people ask me, 'Can you make it better for me?' I say, 'No, because only you know what you feel.' There's no way of making a speech better, if it is completely an expression of your feelings.

Those high-pressure occasions are very easy. The higher the stakes, the easier the speech. Low-pressure situations – say you're the Xerox area manager talking to your Xerox reps about your hopes for sales in the coming months – that is more difficult. Professional obfuscation is totally unnecessary. The ability to make everything simple demands a profound trust in your own knowledge. That analytic skill is unfortunately what is needed to make a good speech. It's about ideas, not an elocution skill, it's not confidence or moving the diaphragm.

Proper preparation for professional performers

David's advice is refreshingly clear. A great speech is simple and heartfelt. It does not demand anything more than preparation, simplicity and passion. I spend much of my professional life helping people with speeches and I've distilled for you the advice that I pass on.

So, how do you come up with what you want to say in the first place?

1. **Put yourself in the shoes of the audience.** The best speeches are written with the audience's needs in mind. If you were listening to you speak, what would you want to hear and how would you want to hear it?

2. **Set your intention for you.** Do you want to make them laugh? Or get a deal?

3. **Set your intention for the audience.**
   - What do you want the audience to *think* about your speech?
   - What do you want them to *feel*? Like a movie director, create a roller coaster of feeling for the audience. Actors know that if you want the audience to feel it, you have to feel it, too.
   - What do you want them to *do*? Standing ovation or worried faces?

4. **Collect stories.** If you have three main points that you want to communicate, all you need is three juicy stories, some links, and you have a speech. Actively collect stories, from newspapers, friends, other speakers. Make the stories relevant to your audience, as well as to you.

5. **Map it out.** Take a big sheet of paper, lots of coloured pens and draw out the journey of the speech as a mind map, with lots of images and colours to free the imagination. Try www.buzanworld.com for mind-mapping tips. If the thought of drawing brings you out in hives, you can also put key ideas and stories on individual stickies and then play with organizing them into a shape. Take a mini version with you into the speech, to put down next to you. Never in your hand though, as it ruins your eye contact!

6. **Rehearsal.** If you want to avoid nerves, you have to practise. You need to feel that you can do the speech without notes in your hand. Above all, you need to know what the links are, so that you can go smoothly from idea to idea, like you would in conversation. When you rehearse make sure that each section has a different energy and pace. Vary the gears so that you keep people awake. Keep it concise and punchy. Less is more. Practise in the mirror – it helps you to see that bigger gestures and facial expressions usually look fine. Rehearse a couple of times at least. If you can, get yourself to the place you're going to be speaking an hour early. Try it out.

7. **Rehearse in your head.** Just in case you have a long journey, or are stuck on some horrible method of public transport, you can achieve a similar effect by visualizing yourself doing it, with what's called 'kin-aesthetic imagery'. It works your brain in almost the same way as doing it for real. In real time you, as the actor, imagine walking slowly out onto the stage, calm and poised. You pause, smile, look out at the audience and start your speech. Run through the whole speech like that, making the moves. This method is used by athletes and musicians to astonishing success. If you have to sit through a long day of speeches before yours you can do it a few times. You'll be amazed how much it can help you.

8. **Relax.** If you tend towards the perfectionist, be careful not to overdo it. Kate Winslet says that over the years she's learned that you can do too much. 'I find myself preparing, preparing, preparing, driving myself mad, post-it notes everywhere, pieces of paper, piles of things. I clutter myself out.' She credits Leonardo DiCaprio with teaching her that there's a point where you have to let it go. 'He says to me, why the stuff? They're all crutches, Kate, just bulls***.' Kate says that Leonardo has 'taught me a hell of a lot about that tricky balance between

preparing and not preparing, or preparing and appearing to have not prepared a thing, having the confidence to throw something out there, let it go.' Prepare to the point where you have the absolute confidence to walk in and let it go. It helps if you don't have too much to carry on the day. Travel light knowing that you have done the work and are ready for anything.

9. **Have fun.** Absolutely crucial! People do speeches every day and enjoy the experience, so lighten up . . . Laurence Olivier was known to suffer from stage fright and turning fear into challenge was one of his tricks for dealing with first nights. He would tell other actors to go to the theatre early, long before the audience has arrived. Then walk out on stage and imagine that the curtain is up. Look out at the imaginary audience and shout, 'You are about to see the greatest performance of your lives. And I will be giving it!'

10. **Be yourself.** Helen Mirren says, '*I found my own way.*' A speech is a reflection of who you are; make it as true to you as you can.

Get onstage, say what you've got to say, and get off

The most valuable thing my father ever said to me was, 'Get onstage, say what you've got to say, and get off.' It's about not indulging . . . I always get to the theatre very early because I love that time. Sit in the dressing room, go down and say hello to the stage. Go back to your dressing room, stretch, go through your script. 'Half hour' – 7:30 to 8:00 – happens, which is sacred time. There is a set routine.

LAURA LINNEY

So much of it is mind over matter. So much of it is about f*** this, you know that I'm going to go out there and show off. If doing that, telling yourself that gets you through, that's OK.

KATE WINSLET

The morning of a speech is when your nerves really come home to roost. Waking up, momentarily you feel light, happy, even carefree. It tends not to last. As hell's mouth opens on the realization that your speech is looming, the rush of butterflies and nausea hits hard. Knowing how to deal with this feeling is crucial if you are to enjoy public speaking. And frankly, far more importantly, if your audience is to enjoy your speech.

Actors are world experts on dealing with performance nerves. It's the hazard of their professional life. Bill Nighy has said that acting is what you do after you get the wind up. If you've ever seen a pony, skittish, jumpy and unpredictable when they feel the wind under their tails, you'll know why that expression is just right for the morning of a speech. You just have to learn to ride the energy.

Hayley Atwell, who has starred in West End shows and Woody Allen films, is an expert on dealing with those last-minute nerves. She's going to help you grab your nerves with both hands and bring them under control, so that you have the courage to walk out onto that stage and shine.

Hayley Atwell

Nerves are natural and I have found it useful to embrace them. When you learn to control your nerves better you can enjoy your performance more. Actually some anxiety can be useful, because nerves, fear and self-doubt can be flipped over to being states of excitement, energy and focus.

There are techniques to help you create this state of focus and excitement, and to settle your mind. Some of these I learned at drama school, particularly in my work with Patsy Rodenburg whose books all offer excellent exercises. They work so well that you can apply them off-stage in daily life when you need to return to a calm centre in stressful situations. If I could use one word on this entire subject it would be 'breathe'.

If I feel that I'm getting nervous before a performance, it helps me to take time to make sure that I own what I'm saying. What I used to do with a speech was to speak it very loudly and very quickly and people would go, 'Oh, you're so confident and impressive.' But I would realize that they hadn't followed what I said, because it was loud, rushed and monotonous. So now, I go off on my own and whisper the words of the speech, almost like I'm sharing a secret with myself. That instantly makes me feel I'm having an intimacy with it. As if I were a child playing, I tell the part of me that is scared and is nervous that it's a game. Then it becomes exciting. I can start to have my own inner connection to the speech and better serve the text to an audience.

Even if you're terrified about starting your speech, you can just take it moment by moment. Surround yourself with what's real. Remain present. I'm sitting in this room. I'm wearing these clothes. My acting partner is picking his nose. One way to take it moment by moment is, as you walk on stage, to take it step by step. It's the Winston Churchill quote of if you're going through hell, keep going. Step by step, you're immediately present. It helps to say to yourself, 'I know if my first line is this, my first word is this, my position on stage is this, I'm just going to get there.'

At drama school I was really scared of the audience and my voice tutor Kate said to me, 'When you get scared and you clam up in the middle of a speech, just love the audience.' It's not about apologizing, or being self-deprecating. If you come back to the audience with compassion you don't feel judged any more.

Love your audience

The concept that love is all you need to give a speech may seem counter-intuitive, but actually it's brilliant. Strictly speaking the feeling we're talking about here is actually compassion. Compassion, or loving-kindness is a state that Buddhists use to meditate on. When you tap into a feeling of compassion for your audience you tap into a creative, productive part of you, freeing you to be yourself in front of an audience.

Some audiences may seem hard to love. If that's the case, visualize a really supportive friend at the back. You can dot a few imaginary friends around the audience, so that you can relax and smile. Talking to individuals softens your energy and makes you more at ease, more natural. Helen Mirren explains, 'Talk as if you're talking to one person. If you imagine one person or five to six people, it becomes, "Hi, how nice to meet you", not "HELLO!" fighting for attention.' It's a tip Helen used herself to get through her Oscars speech, when her global audience was twenty-two million people. It's the same technique that presenters use to camera. They imagine the camera is a friend. It allows you to be more natural, more yourself.

Sometimes, when you're really nervous, love fails you. Under those circumstances, take the f*** you approach. Follow Simon Callow's advice for surviving the terror of first nights: 'a semi-Zen-like state . . . f*** the lot of you, I don't give a s*** what you think, this is good and I'm going to enjoy myself.' Be warned, this will get you through the terror, but it is very much a survival mechanism rather than a route to brilliance. It can create a brittle arrogance, which is why Simon Callow says it's only for first nights. If you need to build a relationship with your audience then compassion will work much better.

Stay in control

A nervous speaker is like a runaway train, going faster and faster until everything is a blur, for them, and for the audience. Ewan McGregor explains, 'Walking up there to start your speech, your heart is in your throat, it's a horrible feeling. Once you start, your temptation is just to speak far too quickly and rattle through what you have to say, and miss bits out. If you can get hold of your nerves and just slow down, think and speak at a reasonable rate, generally it goes all right.' This is easier said than done when you are terrified. Every part of you is saying, go fast, get it over and done with. This is how to do it:

- **Take your time.** When you start, take a moment to look out at the audience in silence. Why? The Greek root of the word mystery is *muein*, which means to close the mouth. When the audience sees you take a silent moment to connect with yourself, and with them, it raises their curiosity about what you have to say, and it makes you seem charismatic and in control. Watch Clinton and Obama – they do it.

- **Pause.** *Spirare* is Latin for breathe. When you pause and wait for your next breath, you 'inspire' your new thought. Try it now: think of your favourite person, and notice that the thought comes in on a new breath. Harness this 'new thought = new breath' principle. When you breathe easy, you allow the relaxed you to show up, rather than the nervous version. Because you convey presence, ease and calm, you relax your audience.

- **Plant your feet.** Make like an oak tree. I don't care that some speakers move around – you have to know how to be still before you can move. Moving your feet can make you feel better – it dispels nerves. But it's very distracting to an audience and makes you unfocused. The movement an audience needs is in your eyes, voice and gesture, not your dancing feet.

- **Make it mean something**. If your nerves threaten to overwhelm you, Jenny Agutter has a great tip. 'If I have to talk to an audience and I'm really nervous, and it's not too formal an occasion, I tell them this means a great deal to me. Then they are aware of where you are, they become receptive. They know you're feeling nervous, because you're passionate about this.' It's a good tip.

- **Go slow.** The best advice for any speaker is as Mark Strong counsels, 'Go slow, because fear makes your voice go higher and faster. Speak slower than you would possibly think you should have to speak.' It sounds obvious but you'd be amazed how rarely people really go slowly enough. Don't confuse pace and energy. You can speak slowly and with great energy. It is when you speed up that you lose the cadence and power. Take your time.

- **Articulate.** 'Be heard' is the first rule of performance. You need to use your speech muscles with focus and energy if you are to make an impact, because an audience connects clear speech with clear thought. It can help to run through some tongue-twisters in advance, to get your speech muscles limber.

- **Project your voice.** Projection is partly psychological, partly technical. Jenny Agutter explains the psychological aspect. 'Projection is about the communication of an idea. You speak the thought to the person clearly and that projects. It's not just about making it loud. You send the thought to where you can see the person, or to the back of the room and you make it land.' However, if you are in a big space, without a microphone, you will also need technique, and it may be useful to see a voice coach for a few sessions. Your voice should never feel strained; projection in a big space is about using the right muscular support for your voice. It's something that you can only learn by doing, and it's well worth seeing an expert.

- **Make every word count.** Dame Edith Evans was once asked by Peter Hall where she placed the emphasis in a speech. She answered, 'I emphasize every word.' What she meant was that you must commit in speech. If it's worth saying, say it fully and with energy. Nerves will make you rush on to the next thought in your mind, while still speaking the previous one. It kills your charisma. Don't do it. Say the thought with *all your energy*. When you have said it, pause. Watch your audience think about it. Hold one thought at a time. You'd never rush a children's story, and as adults we need the same engagement and commitment from our speakers.

- **Use 'jazz hands'.** Gesture really helps you commit. If you use your hands to speak, in a way that reflects exactly what you are saying, then you have to commit fully to each idea. I tell people to use 'jazz hands'. When you gesture fully, all the way to the fingertips, even if the gesture is small, it is committed. Your voice instantly becomes more clear and confident, and your vocal tone becomes rich and more musical. Try it. It works a treat. Palms up is great for openness, and palms down for credibility. If you need emphasis, gesture on the words you want to emphasize.

Above all, the art of a great speech is to remember that it's not about you. While you must *be yourself*, you must not focus *on yourself*. You are there to serve the audience, and to communicate an idea. You must prepare thoroughly and generously, putting your audience's needs first. It is simply good manners to make the speech interesting and relaxed for the audience. Remember the power of compassion for yourself and for them. Be clear, be heard, be passionate, give

The art of a great speech is to remember that it's not about you

the audience something useful, and you've done your job. And enjoy it, because if you care, we do. Have a lovely treat waiting for you when you've finished. You deserve it!

Your toolkit

- **Prepare properly.** Plan like a professional, so that you can do the speech whatever happens, without notes in your hand. Use a mind-map.
- **Quieten your mind.** Be early. Then be quiet. No talking, reading, radio. Sit still and focus on what your audience needs from you. Breathe low and wide. Keep this inner stillness while you are waiting. Listen to the other speakers with full attention and stay relaxed. When you walk out on stage plant your feet. Pause, smile, make a big welcome gesture and you're off. Send the voice to the back of the room, and commit to what you have to say. The more you commit, the better it works.
- **Talk to individuals.** Even if you have an audience of thousands, talk to them as individuals, rather than a sea of scary faces. Use the bumble bee technique. Divide your audience up in to groups of 'flowers'. You speak one thought to each 'flower' at a time. Ensure you send your focus to all different parts of the room/'garden' during the speech. Really see the person you're talking to. When you talk to people, rather than a sea of staring faces you have a lovely chat with friends. It's not scary any more.

CHAPTER 8

Make Your Dream Happen

The road to success is through commitment
and through the strength to drive through that
commitment when it feels hard. It is going to get
hard and you're going to want to quit sometimes.

WILL SMITH

I think everyone has a gift. You just have to be able
to find it and follow your calling. People are afraid to
do that. Some people are afraid of greatness, of success.
And other people are afraid if they try and fail and that
was their one big dream, then what do they have left?

HILARY SWANK

How to Bring Your Dreams to Life

The ability to dream up original ideas and bring your vision to life is an essential star quality. Michelangelo, a true star, tells us, 'The greatest danger for most of us is not that our aim is too high and we miss it, but that it is too low and we reach it.'

So why then, do so many of us have delicious dreams, lying dormant? Why don't we dare to make them happen? Essentially the answer is in the difference between those who daydream and those who do. Peter O'Toole, quoting *Lawrence of Arabia*, explains, 'All men dream: but not equally. Those who dream by night in the dusty recesses of their minds wake in the day to find that it was vanity: but the dreamers of the day are dangerous . . . for they may act their dream with open eyes, to make it possible. This I did.'

Dreams come in all shapes and sizes. You don't have to start with a big dream. Your dream might be to run a marathon, to have the courage to start internet dating, or to persuade people at work to believe in your idea. Go for it.

Making a smaller plan happen is extremely confidence-building and your success will inspire you to keep going.

No matter whether your dream is big or small, you'll benefit from understanding what actors know about vision and motivation. Why? Motivation and imagination are their tools of the trade. An actor uses motivation as a way in to character. Imagination is what inspires them and their audiences, and what they understand about visualization, imagination and thinking big, can help you in life.

If your dream is currently more *wishful thinking* than *wish fulfilment*, fear not. This chapter is all about putting your vision into action. Write yourself into your life script as the protagonist and you may never have to defer a dream again.

What you're going to discover here, over the forthcoming pages, is that the 'dreamers of the day' actually carry out some very simple and effective steps to bring their dreams to life. It's not magic. It's focus, strategy, hard work and a lot of passion.

What's your dream?

I served [in World War II] with men who'd been blown up in the Atlantic . . . The skipper said to me one night, have you any unanswered calls inside you that you

don't understand or can't qualify? I said, well, yes, I
do. I quite fancy myself either as a poet or an actor.
He said, well, if you don't at least give it a try,
you'll regret it for the rest of your life.

PETER O'TOOLE

You see a picture of how you want to be,
even though none of it exists yet. The journey you
have to take to be able to achieve it, the things
you have to believe, it's magic.

WILL SMITH

It was Katharine Hepburn who said that if you don't paddle your own canoe, you don't move. She was so right. When it comes to your dream the big mistake is to hope it will turn up on your doorstep, fully fledged. Life simply doesn't work that way, it's *wishful thinking. Dream fulfilment* takes passion, strategy and, most importantly, action.

Dreams don't make themselves come true. If you want a leading role in your life, then you must write, and act your own script. You may only ever end up with a supporting role unless you clearly define yourself through the way you express yourself, the choices you make, and through the goals you set for yourself – and achieve. No one else can do it for you, and nor should you expect them to.

Write your life script

The first step to making your dream happen is to identify precisely what you want. It sounds obvious, but many wishful thinkers aren't precise enough about this crucial focus. You would never set out on a journey without being clear where you intended to end up. Fulfilling a dream requires similar forethought.

Salma Hayek is a woman who has pursued her dreams both in acting and in production to great success. Interviewed by Oprah, she was clear that the crucial aspect to achieving a dream is in making sure it's really your dream, not what someone else wants for you. 'When we're really young, our dreams are colourful and big and abstract and interesting and imaginative. As the realities of life hit, our dreams become so common. A moment came where I realized what I was doing was not my dream, either . . . And this is one thing I learned: How do you recognize what's your true dream and what is the dream that you are dreaming for other people to love you? The difference is very easy to understand. If you enjoy the process, it's your dream. If you are enduring the process, just desperate for the result, it's somebody else's dream.'

You *must* be clear that it is your dream. There's a Greek word for these dreams of the heart, *autotelic*, from *auto* (self)

and *telas* (goal). Your heart is in autotelic goals and they fill you with the very enthusiasm you will need to sustain you through the inevitable hard times. Any genius you wish to name demonstrates the turbo-fuelled power of an autotelic goal. It's the kind of passion that makes, to paraphrase Noel Coward, work *more fun than fun.*

Second-hand dreams give you blisters

Many people find that their dreams have been squashed by the goals and pressures of school, family and friends. They shrug on other people's goals like ill-fitting second-hand shoes. Warning: Second-hand dreams give you blisters. They are 'exotelic', because they come from outside of us. Society may admire them but they may hold little appeal for you. Second-hand dreams will keep you bound by other people's expectations. If you aren't enjoying the process of working towards a goal, then it's probably not autotelic.

It's easy to get swept up in other people's plans for you if you haven't got your own. 'What's my motivation?' is a theatrical cliché, but it does reflect that an actor must know what is driving the character to act in the way they do. All of us have inner drives. Understanding those drives will help you clarify your goals.

Tony Curtis explains how he learned about the power of motivation early in his career. He was playing a waiter, a small part. It involved one line of dialogue: 'It looks like it's followed you halfway across the country.' Nonetheless, the young Curtis was feeling his nerves as he waited on the set. 'I sat outside that door in my bellhop uniform, I kept running that line over and over again, trying to say it with different words emphasized to see what sounded best: "It *looks* like it's followed you halfway across the country. It looks like it's *followed* you halfway across the country."'

Tony Curtis recounts how his director, Michael Gordon, came to the rescue, reminding him of his character's motivation. It was all he needed to unlock his ability. 'Michael Gordon was watching me. By the door was a red light. When the light went on, that was my cue to knock. I was standing there, getting ready for my shot, thrilled and a little nervous about my big moment . . . I looked to my right and I saw Michael walking toward me. I thought, What's he doing back here? Is he going to walk on with me? He looked at me and said, "How you feeling kid?" "Oh great," I said. He looked at me searchingly and said, "All you want is a tip." Then he turned and walked away. Now Michael couldn't have known I had delivered groceries and shined shoes as a boy.

your dream

But when I worked those jobs that was exactly how I felt. All I wanted was a tip. So I knew just what he meant. How he nailed me with that, I will never know, but it was perfect.'

So, you see, motivation is a simple but devastatingly effective tool for an actor. It's also brilliant for life. The Stoic philosopher Roman Emperor Marcus Aurelius put it succinctly when he said that if you don't know what harbour you're sailing to, no wind is the right wind. When you have a clear goal, you are able to use clement and inclement weather productively, making the most of each situation that presents itself. Rather than floundering, you focus.

How to set goals

The simplest explanation of goal-setting comes from legendary Broadway actress and acting teacher Uta Hagen – though they derive from Stanislavsky. Uta Hagen would ask her actors three simple questions to help them clarify their character's motivation and these same questions work just as well in life.

What do I want? This question focuses you on your ultimate outcome. It's a big question for an actor, when considering character. The character's goal is the line on which the actor threads their actions coherently together. The outcome is clear, the character's steps to get there creates the traffic of the stage. Hamlet wants to avenge his father's death; Billy Elliot wants to dance; Juliet wants Romeo.

When your goal is for your own life, you must be able to see clearly what it is you want to achieve, in your mind's eye. It's why Martin Luther King's dream was so compelling: he could see it clearly, and was able to describe it compellingly to others. What *do* you want? What's your dream? Make a clear picture of something that stirs your soul. It can help to close your eyes and to visualize a movie screen in front of you. On the screen see, in as much detail as you can, how you want to be, making the picture clear, and compelling, with bright colours. Fill it with detail. Who is in the picture? Where are you? What can you hear and see? Make it an inspiring image, one that you will really enjoy working towards.

If it's not easy to make the movie at first, keep practising. Visualization is simply the imagination at work – creating an end result that you can see in your mind's eye. Imagination is a muscle. An actor trains theirs and you can train yours. The more you develop your 'mind's eye' the more creative you become.

What stops me? Once you know your dream, you have to think carefully about what's in your way. You only achieve your goal when you understand how to navigate your way around obstacles.

Pinpoint each obstacle and then find a way to get around them. Billy Elliot has to find a way to persuade his father to let him go to the ballet class. Without that first step, the Royal Ballet is a million miles out of reach. Once he joins the ballet class, Billy is one step closer to his dream.

What do I do to get what I want? When you know your obstacle you can apply your ingenuity. There's a classic acting exercise where someone sits on a chair. The other actor has to persuade them to get off the chair. They can try anything. You see ingenuity at work. They persuade. It doesn't work. They threaten, it doesn't work. They tease. Eventually, because they learn more about the other person and tune in to what works, they find a way to get them to move from the chair.

Achieving a goal takes three elements. You have to know your goal, you have to be aware of the response you're getting, and then you have to flex your behaviour. It was Einstein who said that the definition of insanity was repeating the same behaviour and expecting different results. The secret from acting is that there are a million different ways to achieve a goal. If one way doesn't work, you try something else. This is confidence building, because when you meet obstacles, you know that you are able to respond. If there's something blocking your route to your goal, you find a way around it. Your flexibility is your greatest asset. There's always more than one way to achieve a goal, and you must be ingenious in thinking of the best way to achieve yours.

Stanislavsky talked of the journey to your goal as a railway line. He advised laying out each track you need in order to travel down the line. Of course, you'll help yourself to stay on track if you make the journey as fun as you can. Give yourself what Stanislavsky called 'attractive objectives which loom ahead of us'. Then, get going.

Make the journey as fun as you can

The beauty of working with an actor's system for motivation is that it is about *doing* rather than *thinking*. Once enrolled in ballet class Billy's steps are to attend classes and to practise. The steps are often mundane and repetitive, but that is the reality of any dream fulfilment. You have to do the work and you have to find the discipline to do the work. Stanislavsky told his actors, 'After you have laid your rails of objectives, get aboard and start off to new lands . . . You will be moving along, not staying in one place . . . you will take *action*.' Chart your direction towards your autotelic goal and you will discover that enthusiasm fuels your engine, powering you along, even when times get tough.

Find physical freedom

Once you have are clear on the dream, you must find a way find a way to voice your brilliant idea so that others listen. Much of the impact you have when you express your dream to others is physical and vocal. Your physical intelligence must be nurtured as much as your creative intelligence. There's nothing new in this – Michelangelo was described by the his-torian Vasari as being in possession of great poise and physical prowess. In a sedentary society we are in danger of forgetting how interconnected physicality and creativity are. Actors cannot – because their work is about creativity and physicality combined. Here Anna Massey talks about the power of balancing work on mind and body.

Anna Massey

If you've got something passionate to say and there's a will behind you then you will find the means to express it. Talent that wants to be heard is a powerful force. Obama found his voice. He's physically incredibly free . . . he kept incredibly fit during that gruelling seventeen months of the campaign. You must work on the body as you work on the mind. If you've got a very consti-pated set of vocal cords you must find some way to lubricate them. Some people are ramrod stiff and that's important to work through. If you're physically free as well as mentally free you're going to be better at your profession. Your imagination is allowed to run riot.

In an increasingly sedentary world we'd all do well to take Obama's example and remember the importance of flexibility in movement as well as thought. They are inseparable. Find a physical discipline you enjoy and develop your skills, recog-nizing that the mind and body work in unison.

Pitch your vision

I tell my children, if you lay down people will step over you, but if you keep scrabbling, if you keep going, someone will always, always give you a hand. Always, but you've got to keep dancing.

MORGAN FREEMAN

The best analogy that I've ever come up with [for theatre]
is that it's like anybody who plays sports or plays chess.
Every time you play, it's a new game – every time. The
rules are the same. But the game is new.

KEVIN SPACEY

There's no magic trick to turning your dream into action. When you spend too much time in wistful contemplation you are wishing your dream away. Many once-brilliant ideas and big dreams now languish in drawers. If you want to prevent your big dream going down this pitiful route you need to move it forward. Get out of the abstract and into action.

Get out of the abstract and into action

If your idea is to see the light of day, you're going to need support from others. To persuade the right people you have to be able to pitch to perfection. A good pitch is about expressing your brilliant idea with passion and clarity so that others can understand its brilliance and what it offers them.

You may want to get a film off the ground, raise money for a good cause, or find investors for a business. Whatever you're pitching, understand that people have to trust you and like you for them to help you. Your job is to persuade them that you are worthy of an investment of their time and/or money.

You need what Aristotle called 'pathos' – the ability to persuade your audience to warm to you. This requires alert antennae. You will need to gauge the mood of the room and adjust with precision to the ever-shifting responses of your audience.

Actors are experts when it comes to audience response. Each night of a show is different, depending on the mood of the house. Actors know about this sensitivity: a matinee audience full of schoolchildren is very different from a revved-up Friday-night house. An actor develops a sixth sense about the audience and adjusts their energy accordingly.

Damian Lewis is a good adviser to help you make your mark in a pitch. He has had direct experience of successfully pitching to Hollywood with his production company. He knows how it works, and talks here about using an actor's understanding of performance to pitch successfully.

Damian Lewis

There's a sort of genius in having the wherewithal, having the chutzpah, the far-sightedness and the confidence to take your vision to people. I think it's as simple and as complicated as that.

You have to burn bright with an idea and then have the vision and self-possession to convey it and the energy to stimulate and pro-voke people. The people who can do it are out there succeeding, ground-breaking and boundary-pushing.

Promoting oneself and promoting an idea are two very differ-ent things. Promoting an idea is a far less thorny path. I'm happy to pitch to a hundred people. I only need one person to like it, it's all you need. You hopefully won't have to go through a hundred but there are so many factors at play. It's about the complex nature of personalities.

You can't impose a formula, because it needs to come from you organically. People love stories, and that's the crucial ele-ment. If your story's a good story and if they're excited by it, then you've got half a chance. It's important to know your story very well, so you can tell it concisely. Be passionate and able to enthuse about it. Find what is amusing, harrowing, moving, whatever it happens to be. Particularly find one or two moments in the pitching of the story where you can bring in a bit of humour. It becomes a performance in itself, knowing the timing of it. It's rather like telling an anecdote; pause before the punch-line.

The people you're pitching to are execs, hard-bitten number-crunchers. They're already doing the maths during the pitch. They're thinking, 'Where can we place this? How do we market that? Who can be involved in this?' They're piecing it all together, in a rather more technical way. But they will only respond to stories that they like, I'm convinced of that. They need content, they need new stories. In those fifteen to twenty minutes that you have together in a room, you're trying to infect someone with your enthusiasm and the love of your own story.

You can't be 'on' all the time. Sometimes your pitch has greater fluency than other times. You know when you have a willing audience, rather than someone who's sat back in their chair and squeezed you in for a few minutes in the day and they really just want to go home and see their kids. It's like a live theatre audience, some people need persuading, and some are willing participants. You have to gauge it in the room as best you can. It's always telling if someone turns their phone off. Then you've got a good chance, they're focused and they're committed to hearing your ideas.

When a good pitch works, you infect the audience with your enthusiasm. This is essential to grasp, precisely because most people make the mistake of worrying about the words and the visuals and forget entirely that it's the emotion that matters. Why? Emotion, not logic persuades. Great orators have understood this since ancient times. Your logic must be *impeccable* and then your emotion gives it impact.

If you only think about what you say when you rehearse your pitch, you're missing a trick. If a great pitch were only about content, then you would simply send it on email. That's not how it works, because your audience are as interested in you as they are in what you have to say. Your energy and presence will persuade them as much as your ideas, whether you like it or not.

You have a lot of work to do before the pitch if you want to have impact. There is no magic trick. To paraphrase Stanislavsky, rehearsal is the only way to make the difficult habitual, the habitual easy, and the easy beautiful. As you plan your content you must remember that every single person in your audience will be asking themselves the question, 'What's in it for me?' You only deserve their interest when you can tell them.

Be sure that you are ready. Your idea needs to be sufficiently distilled and clear that you can summarize its unique hook in one sentence. It's your 'elevator pitch' – you can persuade someone to back you in the time it takes to travel between floors. If you can't explain it in a sentence you're not ready.

How to communicate your vision

You also need to be very clear on your vision. Once you have decided on your own inner motivation, the art of a pitch is how to communicate that vision compellingly to an audience so that they can understand the win for them. What will your idea look like when it happens? How can you tell that story in a way that compels and excites your audience? Like telling a story to a child, you have to walk with your audience, taking them on a journey with you. See how it looks from their eyes. What do they need to know at each stage of the pitch? Don't overload them, keep it simple. Plot the stories and pictures you want to express, and practise expressing them concisely and passionately.

You need an exact idea of how you want your audience to feel. Think about the emotional journey. Are you going to start with calm credibility, then curiosity, followed by excitement? Or do you want them to feel worried, then thoughtful, then passionate? When you realize the power of emotion, you become like a movie director, taking the audience on a compelling emotional journey through your ideas.

You need to be clear on how you want your audience to feel

The simplest, most honest, and thus most affecting way to generate emotion in others is to ensure that your pitch involves ideas you feel strongly about. If you want the audience to feel passionate, talk about your passion for the idea. When your passion converges with a win for your audience, you will persuade. If you want them to be intrigued, what intrigues you? If you need to communicate fear, what frightens you? Fear can be a powerful motivator as long as you lead people somewhere positive afterwards.

Don't even contemplate faking it. It's horribly cheesy and deeply unimpressive. Only truth of emotion communicates in performance. The worst possible thing you can do is to force a big performance when you don't feel it. The effort looks desperate, and it alienates your audience. You need to take them with you, not push them away.

Taking your audience with you also involves you reading the room and responding to it. Anna Massey explains, 'With an audience your eye and your ear needs to be in more than one place at a time. You have to be aware of them and play ball with them. It lights up then. Suddenly, you say something and they are on your wavelength. If you're too much "in" you're excluding your audience. It is to be shared.'

Being 'in' happens when your focus is too much on yourself. Worrying too much about what you're saying or how you're perceived is a selfish act in performance. 'Generous' is a word you hear used a lot by actors. It is mocked as being rather thespian by those who don't know much about acting, but it is actually *crucial* to good performance. Generous performers aren't worrying about their hair, their delivery or their tax bill. Their focus is on the audience. If you want natural easy presence in a pitch you must give your audience *at least* 60 per cent of your attention and energy.

To be able to read the room you must also be like an actor, 'off the book', without notes in hand. Ewan McGregor explains, 'You need to have thought through all the points you want to cover and then allow yourself the luxury of thinking through them as you speak.' If you're remembering lines in your head, your eyes go dead. Don't do it. If you take your time, you only need to hold one thought at a time. This lightens the pressure and makes the experience more relaxing for everyone concerned. It's not a memory test, it's a conversation.

To persuade your audience you also need to *feel* your pitch in your solar plexus. You can only do that one thought at a time. The mistake that people make is to try to hold the whole pitch in their head, and do it all at once. Don't. Do it thought by thought.

How do you achieve this? One breath at a time. As long as you know your intention for the meeting: they ask if you can call them, they give you their card, they look excited (all good early wins), you can work step by step. You take in their response, and you work out what they need to know next, and how you want them to feel. If you want your audience to feel excited, pause, take in the thought, feel the excitement on the in-breath, speak on the out-breath. Throw the thought out to the audience and watch them catch it. Be curious as to how they respond to the thought. Their response will inform what you say next.

Pauses matter more than anything in a pitch. The pitch *happens* in your pauses, because that's when your audience is responding in their heads, making their minds up about you. It's absolutely imperative that you give them time to do that.

Many people ask actors how they keep a performance alive night after night. It's not easy, and you can have precisely the same challenge with a pitch, if you have to pitch to many different people. Even if you have done the pitch one hundred times, as far as your audience is concerned, each time must be the first. The art is to recognize that *Each audience demands a completely different approach* each audience demands a completely different approach. The pitch actually happens in the dynamic space *between* you and the audience. When you are able to respond fully to them, each pitch *is* different. This ability to respond in the moment keeps great performers electric, even in a six-month run, and it can keep your passion alive in your pitch.

Finally, be stoic about the fact that you can't control everything. Understand that there are social dynamics at play that are not about you. If it's 8 a.m. and your audience is grouchy, it's not personal, but you do need to adjust to their energy level. Take it slowly, sip coffee, ease them into the pitch. If it's late in the day and they have to catch a flight, be punchy, precise and concise. They're not likely to warm to you if you make them late. A good pitch is as much about the trust and enthusiasm that brings individuals together, as it is about an idea. Your awareness of your audience needs to reflect that in every pitch you do. Put the people first.

Difficult is good

I have a phrase which I taught my children . . .
Use the difficulty . . . Where I came from nobody
knew what drama school was, and everybody thought
you couldn't become an actor unless you talked posh.

MICHAEL CAINE

There's a great Joseph Papp line. 'The only definition
for success is how you handle your disappointment.'

ETHAN HAWKE

Thinking big isn't easy. If it was, everybody would be doing it. The reason that most people don't turn their dreams into reality is because they want to protect themselves. Wishful thinking is a get-out clause – wish your life away and you never have to take action.

Putting your vision to the test is difficult, but it can offer excitement that wishful thinkers can only dream of. Imelda Staunton talks here about using difficulties and setbacks to move forward in life so you can cope when things go wrong, as they will.

Imelda Staunton

Life is hard and a lot of people are obsessed with making it easy. It doesn't have to be easy. Hard is good. Difficult is good. Failure is good. We learn from failure. That's how you start to form armour – you have to protect yourself.

As an actor, not many people protect you. Your agents don't say, 'Well, you've done these jobs, now you have to do something different.' No one moulds you. You have to do that yourself. That's what I quite like about the job. You have to do everything. In society we tend to want people to do things for us. It's better just to get on and do it.

At the same time you have to protect yourself, to be kind to your-self, not to give yourself too hard a time. It's just a little kit you've got to get together and some days it will work and some days it won't. Some days the cut is deeper and you don't have a plaster for it.

217

You have to have resilience, to get up, get going, go. You have to have perseverance. And you have to be honest with yourself. Year One: Do you mind being rejected? Do you want to keep doing this job? Yes I do. Year Two: Do you want to keep doing this? Yes I do. Year Seven: Do you want to keep doing this? And also you need to be able to recognize, it's been seven years and I haven't really done anything. Maybe I should move on, maybe I should do something else. If it's seven years and you haven't worked, don't waste your life.

There'll be many days when it's not your turn. There will be days when it *is* your turn. That doesn't mean that everything is going to be successful in life. Not everything is successful and we don't always get what we want.

You have to find an inner person to help you through. To say, I am good enough. Or to realize, obviously, I'm not good enough and I need to move on. You have to be very honest with yourself.

It's not to do with pride. Pride has to go out of the window. You have pride in your work but not in your own ability. The minute you start looking at your ability, start thinking you're really good, it all goes tits up. You're no better than the next person at any given moment so the most important thing is to recognize that you're there in the service of something bigger than you.

I agree entirely with Imelda: difficult *is* good. When you embrace the difficult your creativity is tested. If you succeed, your confidence will enjoy a growth spurt. Psychologists call the ability to adapt in adverse circumstances, 'transformational coping'. If you are resourceful, humble, open and flexible, then you stand a good chance of turning a bad situation into a better one.

Thinking big can be a long road and it helps to see challenges in a broader time-span. It took years for Morgan Freeman to break through in his acting career. He was about to give it all up to drive a cab: 'I would have quit years ago, because it was hard . . . What you're going for it's really difficult, it's like climbing Everest. Only a few are going to get there. Those who are willing to overcome it, are going to overcome. Mostly it's just yourself, doubts and fears, insecurities . . . You're going at it, you're going at it, you're going at it, you don't see the results. You don't see anything coming back. And then every now and then something comes along, just when you're ready to fall off the edge of the cliff, something comes up, you'll keep going.'

Doing the best with the resources that you've got is a founding principle of theatre. Actors learn to expect – and welcome – the unexpected. A good test of an actor is how they respond when the glass of wine spills on stage, or an actor exits too early. A good actor takes it all in their stride and reacts to whatever comes their way, without letting it throw them. It's the mark of a professional. Oscar-nominated

Amy Adams explains, 'I just acknowledge everything that's going on and figure out a way to use it . . . that comes from working in dinner theatre, because you're like, "OK, that person just put their potato on the stage, what am I going to do?" It's all about accomplishing your goal within the parameters of the space you're working in.'

What actors learn is that the answers are all around you if you pay attention. The worst thing you can do is isolate yourself when you hit a challenge. It's so tempting to curl up and hide, but that's a bad option. If you keep your eye on the big picture, you'll realize that the answer to your problem is out there, if you stay alert to the possibilities. Look for the clues and signs that will help you, or show you that you are on (or off) track. Even when you can't see much coming back for your efforts, keep going and stay open. When you do get positive feedback you can use it to move you forward.

You also have to keep stoking the fire that created the dream in the first place. Tom Hanks has talked of his 'fallow year' of unemployment as a young actor in LA. Tom explains that the secret to perseverance 'is like a love affair with something you're going to do for the rest of your life. You have to protect what it is you love.' Keep developing your skills and your passion for your trade. Openness, enthusiasm and humility open doors where pride, bitterness and a closed mind slam them shut.

A word of caution about goals. There's a very fine balance between staying focused and being fixated. When you're too single-minded it's not good for you. Don't get too hooked on the final destination that you forget to enjoy the journey. Make the most of each step on the journey, and appreciate how far you've come, as well as how far you've got to go. Be clear on your ultimate purpose and then be flexible when it comes to your *modus operandi*.

The next time you hit a brick wall en route to your dream, as you will, don't waste time beating yourself up. Take responsibility. Don't wait for someone to come to the rescue, because no one is going to rescue you. Be kind to yourself and know that challenges and obstacles are part of life. Sit down and take a close look at your situation. Are you on track? Have you come off the rails? Is the goal the right goal for you? You have to trust your gut. If you've stopped enjoying the process, then the goal may need to change. If you're still enjoying the process, keep at it, all is well.

There's a very fine balance between staying focused and being fixated

The world runs on the fuel of people with big dreams and the chutzpah to bring them to life. Where would the world be if Martin Luther King had decided not to tell anyone about his dream? Where would we be if Emmeline Pankhurst had decided that getting the vote for women was too ambitious? Don't leave your dream to wishful thinking: Act on it.

Your toolkit

- **Make the dream yours.** Make sure the goal is yours. The only dreams that really mean anything to you are your own. If it's someone else's dream, you may not find the passion you need to make it happen.

- **Make your movie.** Big dreams demand compelling visions. It has to be great for you to want to work towards it. Walt Disney had a useful strategy. He would encourage his creatives to separate their creative thinking in three ways, after first moving into different physical spaces to think. Try it, move to a different place (a chair/room will do) for each thinking style. The three thinking styles were:

  1. **Dreamer** – This is about vision: be creative and inspired. Think big.
  2. **Realist** – This is practical. How, physically, will you do it? Think of your steps, your action.
  3. **Critic** – Ask yourself, what could go wrong? Analyse your obstacles, think your way past them.

- **Sell your idea.** How you tell your story in the pitch matters enormously. The art of pitching is the art of great storytelling. Get good at it. Watch stand-up comics and professional storytellers in action. Learn their tricks. Learn to tell jokes. Work out how to pause before the punchline, how they emphasize and use tone and pace.

• **Fail again, fail better.** If you feel disillusioned by an early lack of success, read autobiographies. It will help you realize that none of the greats found success easily, and knowing that can give you the fuel to keep going.

CHAPTER 9

Bounce Back

Embrace adversity with all you have. It is the greatest teacher you can ever encounter if you embrace it and learn from it.

SALMA HAYEK

You have to have a balance of crazy belief in yourself, also a very informed objectivity.

GLENN CLOSE

How to Handle Vulnerability, Criticism and Rejection – and Keep Going

Dreams don't always come true. Sometimes serendipity doesn't show up. Dark days come, leaving you feeling vulnerable, rejected and criticized. They're never going to be pleasant, but there are ways of soothing the pain. When you are able to bounce back from troubled times, you demonstrate the star qualities of resilience and endurance. How you deal with rejection and vulnerable moments says so much more about you than how you deal with success.

Actors know about vulnerability. Many people don't fully realize quite how competitive and challenging the acting profession is. It has some unique psychological pressures, and some unique ways of dealing with them, which can be of use to all of us in our own moments of challenge.

Actors put their very soul up on stage and screen for public judgement and those in work consider themselves to be a very fortunate breed. Most actors experience the heart-breaking cycle of audition and rejection, more than they experience the euphoria of getting work. Actors' union Equity has estimated that 70 per cent of actors are out of work at any one time. Legendary theatre actor Ralph Richardson put it beautifully when he said, 'Actors have much in common with taxi drivers. After each run we put up a for-hire sign, and always fear that we may never get another fare.'

In order to survive actors must develop grace and equanimity in the face of difficult news. Their advice, crash-tested in the toughest of circumstances, is also a great tonic for you to use in your own life because they know first-hand the sting of rejection for a job they really want, or the hurt of a critic's jibe. Most importantly they know how to stay serene in these most challenging of situations. Contrary to stereotype, divas are not welcomed in the pressured environment of a film set or rehearsal space. Kick up a fuss, and word soon gets round that you are unprofessional – a career death blow.

All actors must have a suit of armour for resilience; and a soft underbelly for sensitivity. The suit of armour shields you from attack. Underneath it, your soft underbelly gives you intuition, imagination, empathy and openness to new experience. The training in a leading drama school is a combination of almost military levels of focus and discipline, with the playfulness needed to tease out creativity. If you are five minutes late to your first class you are shut out for the rest of the day. In some drama schools the rule is then three strikes and you're out.

This temperament is of benefit whatever your discipline. The good news is, you can learn it. This chapter is about giving you a suit of armour for vulnerable times, pushed to the back of the wardrobe when it's not required. Why? Because you mustn't let fear of failure, rejection or criticism stop you living your life. It's wiser to save the emotion for a true emergency. Your emotions are there to help you, not limit you. If you can

You mustn't let fear of failure, rejection or criticism stop you living your life

overcome your anxieties you can find the self-possession that makes for star quality. Those who are able to develop this tough mental and emotional discipline also develop grace.

These qualities are all star qualities, and will be of support in any situation where you meet those unpleasant obstacles of rejection and criticism, or the sudden pain of vulnerability.

Feel comfortable with vulnerability

You can be singing along, thinking everything is fine, then the rain clouds and the lightning can just sweep in, and you can find yourself devastated. Depressed. You can make bad decisions. If you find

yourself getting worked up and agitated over things
that aren't big picture it's just destructive.

UMA THURMAN

You have to have light and shade. They are both
important and you have to be able to balance
them. You have to admit that sadness is part of
you and that it enriches you.

IMELDA STAUNTON

Vulnerability is a devious creature. You can be having a perfectly lovely time until one small thing avalanches you over the precipice. A call, an email, a sideways glance can be all it takes to shake you to your core. This advice is for those days.

Eve Best is going to help you get through your vulnerable moments with courage. Eve knows all about emotion, having played tragic characters such as Hedda Gabler on the London stage. She has starred with leading men Kevin Spacey, Ian McShane and Jude Law in great theatres such as the Old Vic, the National Theatre and on Broadway. Imagine playing a tragedy, traversing the darkest lows and the highest highs of the human psyche. In one night.

Eve talks about how to accept your vulnerability and to minimize it, with an actor's understanding of the body/brain connection. It will help you manage your emotion with humility and dignity. It's all part of your star quality.

Eve Best

It's a constant battle isn't it? One day you feel OK and the sun's shining. Suddenly the next day you've crashed into something, lost your life belt. You're drowning and you're terrified and you feel vulnerable. Everything's wrong, a black itchy horrible mess. You start imploding and the world starts exploding.

In *True or False* [award-winning playwright David Mamet's book on acting], David Mamet says, 'Everyone I know feels like a fraud.' In any situation, ten to one, absolutely everyone in the room is feeling vulnerable – even the most confident person. It's liberating when you realize that so many people in the world feel that way, and are terrified of it. The secret is learning how to accept vulnerability, to feel comfortable with it. All you want as a child and as a grown-up is to be given that permission to be vulnerable. I was in the park with some friends and their child. At first he was very accepting of me, we had a lovely time. Then he began to play on his own and he was clearly feeling increasingly vulnerable. He turned to me and suddenly, having been very friendly, he walks over and says, 'That's *my* mum . . . you don't speak to her.' Instead of reprimanding him, telling him to be quiet, or ignoring him, his mother asked him, 'What's going on? What are you feeling?' The child didn't have the vocabulary to express it. So his parents said, 'Are you feeling jealous?' and the child said, 'Yes.'

Then, everybody knows that he's been hostile and rude only because he's feeling vulnerable and left out. It's totally understandable. As a result we include him and are able to carry on with our conversation. He has been given permission from the parents to feel vulnerable and told that that's OK. We change our behaviour and then he feels safe again.

You don't need to feel anything else than what you're feeling right now. It's powerful to be able to say, 'I feel vulnerable, uncomfortable, unsafe.' As soon as you can say it, and acknowledge it, you are able to do something about it. You're not a victim any more, because you're aware of what's happening to you. Then, even if there's no one else around, at least you can say to yourself, 'OK, OK, stop, stop.'

Writing can help. Make a list of the things that are wrong. It gives your brain some sort of order, gets it out of your skin. You can then see it as a small thing.

Finding something physical to do is important, too. Get back in touch with the physical world. Focusing on the outer can get you out of the inner. I always forget to do it myself! If you're having a row with somebody, leave and go and have some fresh air, water, whatever. Whenever I have to do my tax I put on a pair of high heels and a short skirt. Then I feel like I'm the secretary, I'm in my office. It's important, it's the exterior affecting the interior.

It's quite often a good idea to change your physicality – even as simply as by looking up. Your frame of mind is completely different if you look down. If you look at the skyline, just the physical act of looking up, opens you up. Whereas looking down closes you down. Most of the time we walk down the street, we've got our heads down. I'm sure it's why one's frame of mind is so different when you travel. New York seems open to me because it's new. When I'm there I look up. If you feel fear, or vulnerability, try it, look up.

There's a reason why we describe people as being 'down in the dumps', why we tell our friends to 'keep your chin up'. You can adjust your emotion through your physicality.

This is useful to know. When you understand the actor-world understanding of the body-emotion connection, you realize that all emotion is OK. You don't need to inhibit emotion: you accept it, knowing that you don't need to stay there, unless you want to. In fact all emotion is good. Just as fear keeps you safe, sadness and vulnerability can help you to move forward if you accept them.

The secret to vulnerability is to notice how it affects your body as much as your brain. Acting teacher Viola Spolin advised that vulnerability was best dealt with by 'giving . . . full head-to-toe attention to what is going on around you right now . . . then you are no longer fragmented and disconnected . . . fear dissolves.' Vulnerability likes you to time travel in your head. It particularly loves to feed on the guilt it finds in your past and the anxieties you have about your future.

Fight vulnerability by bringing your attention back to what's actually happening right now. Underneath all the worrying is a very calm version of you, right at your core. While you're stressing out, it watches quietly. It's always been there, and it always will be there. All you have to do is allow yourself to pay attention to it. If you sit still, turn off the phone and the email, relax your shoulders, close your eyes, you tune in to this calm you.

There's science to support this. A Cambridge University study showed that taking time to notice how you are feeling, right now, could reduce depression by 50 per cent. Another study showed that tuning in to your emotions prevents weight gain, because it regulates the mood swings that lead to comfort eating. As Meryl Streep puts it, 'Living in the moment is the whole point.' When you stop spinning around in your head you realize that the present moment is always there, if you take time to notice it. It's a 'present' that

Living in the moment is the whole point

you can give yourself whenever you want to. You don't have to do anything to find it, all you have to do is *stop doing and pay attention.*

The simplest way to start? Pay attention to your breathing. Feel the air come in, and go out. The art to breathing is to do as little as possible. Heaving your shoulders up and down is hard work, and makes you more stressed. You breathe best when you're asleep.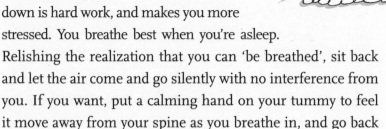

Relishing the realization that you can 'be breathed', sit back and let the air come and go silently with no interference from you. If you want, put a calming hand on your tummy to feel it move away from your spine as you breathe in, and go back to your spine as you breathe out.

Another way to get you out of head-bound anxiety, and relax you into the calm of the body, is through movement. The next time you feel vulnerable, move, shift position, go for a walk. Look up at the sky like Piglet rather than down at the floor like Eeyore. Jump around Tigger-style. Let the 'outer affect the inner', and find your momentum again. Once you get moving everything flows. As Will Smith puts it, 'As long as you keep moving, things are going to shake out . . . Things are going to adjust.'

Bounce back from rejection

*With success comes rejection and disappointment,
too. Matthew [Broderick] and I, we've both had
a lot of disappointments, even if it may not look like that
from the outside. Sometimes all you can do is say, 'Well,
you know, we have each other, we have this wonderful
son, we have our health.' We do all of that to get our
brains to focus on the positive, but it's hard, it's really
hard. Whether you're an actor, an artist, a teacher or a
doctor, the only thing you can do with disappointment
and failure is live it. Don't deny it. You invested a lot
of time and a lot of heart in something and it's OK
to feel this way. But then you simply have to have
the constitution to move on.*

SARAH JESSICA PARKER

*You learn that the first failure isn't the end. I thought
I'd seen the end of my career ten times over. I've
experienced them as death blows. What's nice – after
numerous efforts, successes, failures, losses, professional
and personal – is to actually accept you're not going
to ace your life. You suffer, then you get on with it.*

UMA THURMAN

Rejection is a vicious little thing. It gets you right below the belt. The trick is to get straight back up again. Down but not out. That resilience is what helps you make your own luck. Knowing you can bounce back helps you to see rejection for what it is, a great test of your mettle. Knowing you can cope at the worst of times gives you the backbone to deal with success when it comes. That's why it's such an important star quality.

Minnie Driver talks here about the ways in which actors learn to overcome the inevitable rejections they all face as part of the daily realities of their profession. Her advice to you will help you to deal better with your own dark moments of rejection, and fight back to achieve the success you deserve.

Minnie Driver

Rejection is a real beast of a problem. You cannot admit it into your soul, you just can't. In those dark moments, you have to collect yourself and that's about creating space. You immediately feel a wallop in your stomach, you feel everything tightening, you think you're shit. In that moment it feels like all the air's been sucked out of the room and out of your life, and there's nothing to be done.

First of all that's not the truth, because you're still there with your heart beating and your breath, and everything is fine, but you need to remember that. When you get shaken by it to the point that it makes you incredibly sad or incredibly angry, they've won in a way. Your wellbeing cannot be based on the approbation of others. The best thing to do is to keep reconnecting with what you believe, what *you* think the truth is.

I give myself half an hour to feel rage. To scream, whatever it is I'd like to scream at that disgusting person. And then to think, this is just another human being with an opinion, and I am a human being with my opinion. Rejection or failure is disempowering ultimately, so you have to find ways to empower yourself again.

I honestly believe that requires removing myself from other people, sitting quietly, breathing and checking in with everything that is really, really, really good in my life, being grateful. At one time I was down to: my family loves me; my legs work; I'm going swimming tomorrow; I've got fifty quid left; I'm fine for a couple of days and I'm going to get a job. Bring your mind back not to the stuff that isn't happening, but the stuff that is. It's incredibly galvanizing.

Stop. Breathe. Take stock. Don't be terrified. Connect with what is good. It makes you feel better and the minute you feel better, things can start to shift again. I knew I'd get there in the end if I just didn't shut off any avenues. You can become your very own worst enemy.

I'd wanted to be an actress so profoundly, from a very young age. I'd heard about the National Youth Theatre and, at the age of fourteen, this suddenly became this incredibly important step in my life. I prepared and I studied and went to London for an audition and was terrified. I waited and I didn't get it. I was completely devastated.

There was a really wonderful guy, he was an old boy at my school, who sat me down and said, 'Look, there's no dishonour or trouble in losing the race, there's only dishonour and trouble when you didn't run it because you were afraid to lose. You're ahead. You're ahead because you identified something that you wanted to do and you set your course, you went towards it. Even though you didn't have the outcome you'd anticipated, it had its own merits.' At fourteen that was hard to understand, but it's an enduring and really beautiful lesson, that the doing might not always turn out the way you think it should, but so long as you're doing, you're moving forward.

What I like about Minnie's advice is that she doesn't tell you to pretend the rejection hasn't happened. This isn't about denial. It's about turning the energy into something productive. Let rejection hit you – scream if you want to. Then do something about it.

It's not about pretending to be happy. Being rejected is horrible, there's no getting around that. Rufus Sewell put it perfectly when he told me that, 'It's probably best to be philo-sophical, but it's inevitable with rejection, you're going to take it personally. What happened to me I think is that though my skin is just as thin as it ever was, it just regenerates quicker. I'm just as easily hurt and disappointed but within a day now I'm like oh, whatever. There's such a tapestry of experience of rejection behind me and enough experience to know that there is no rhyme or reason to it. You could come back three inches taller and they still wouldn't want you.'

However much you're hurting there's still something you can do. When you least feel like it you must pull yourself up by the bootstraps and find *something* to be positive about.

The problem with rejection is that it triggers what Viola Spolin called the problem of success/failure thinking. She blamed the rush to succeed, saying that it can lead you to give in to failure when you get rejected, 'draining precious energy, weakening our very life force'. Failure thinking makes you say things to yourself, like 'I'm a loser', 'I'll never make it'. You mustn't give into this victim mind-set.

Find something to be positive about

Don't let rejection shut you in a gloomy tunnel of despair. All you notice is more rejection, discontent and despair. You have to find a way to tunnel out, letting in a chink of sunshine to light up your life. Even if, as Minnie said, you're down to:

my family love me, I have fifty quid and I'm going swimming tomorrow. It's a good start . . .

Anna Massey is stoic about overcoming dark moments. 'If I feel pessimistic I just think of my grandchildren having tea in Dorset and throwing things on the floor. You just live from day to day, hour to hour with the people that you care about in focus and that can feed you. You only find people if you're open. You can go through life blinkered, not ever meet any-one, because one's so self-involved, fearful, pessimistic, all the negatives.'

What we're talking about here is the practice of gratitude. Gratitude has its roots in the Latin word *gratia* meaning grace. Grace is exactly what it gives you. Johnny Depp has said that spending time with Romany gypsies taught him a lot about appreciating what he has. 'Those guys really knew the definition of living, not in terms of a constant party. They lived every single moment. You forget what a gift every single breath that you're given is. We never pay respect to that, but they appreciate every moment, every breath they take, every move . . . well, you know the song.'

Science agrees that gratitude is a powerful mindset. Dr Robert Emmons and Dr Michael McCullough at Cambridge University found that the regular practice of grateful thinking showed an increase in happiness levels by more than 25 per cent. So, take Minnie's advice. When it gets bad take a moment to list all the things that are going well for you. Even better, write it down. In the same study, those who kept gratitude journals for three weeks felt better about their health, slept more and exercised an hour and a half more on average.

The lovely side-effect to gratitude is that, as Minnie has told you, it 'de-calcifies' you, frees you to build yourself back up in other parts of your life. It's something that Frances McDormand believes is crucial. 'I always say to younger

Ever tried, ever failed. Fail, fail again, fail better

people when they ask my advice, that the most important thing to practise is *not* working. How *not* to let one's work identify you so that when there is no work, and there will often be no work, you still have interests, friends and activities that keep you aloft and exploring until the next work opportunity presents itself.'

Remember, life is a long game. You do best to take playwright Samuel Beckett's advice: 'Ever tried, ever failed. Fail, fail again, fail better.' Scratch any successful actor and you will find a history of terrific disappointments. An absolute foundation stone of star quality is the ability to bounce back from rejection.

Do remember to keep your eye on the goal. As long as you know where you're headed you will find creative ways around your obstacles. Spolin said, 'If you have a focus you will not be engulfed in fear, or lose access to intuition, the energy source needed to solve the problem.' If it takes ten 'no's to get to a 'yes', then all you can do is treat each rejection as one step closer to your goal. Treat each hurdle as the great learning experience that it is. Really – even the hardest knocks, they are the most useful.

Keep criticism in perspective

I've got this dread of criticism. Especially from people I admire. Part of me shies away from the notes they may give me, but part of me is grateful because I can learn from them.

ANNA MASSEY

You just say sometimes people will like it and sometimes people won't like it. What's most important is if you've done work that you think is the best you could possibly do – at the time, with the tools you have, you do the best you can.

GLENN CLOSE

Listening to criticism is hard. Most people run away from the mere thought of being criticized. They create an impenetrable suit of defensiveness which prevents them from growing.

Actors know that no one is too big or too smart to do without criticism. In your life the same is true. Criticism is a powerful force for growth if you can stay open to it. It's a bit like going to the dentist. It's not exactly pleasant, and you need to actively calm yourself down to cope with it. But you need the dentist's expertise to counteract the rot that can set in if you leave it be. We all have habits and faults that we ourselves don't notice. Having them pointed out is painful but usually necessary.

Even legends stay open to criticism from people they respect. Anna Massey tells the story of Sir John Gielgud. 'When he was in his late, late years, coming on for ninety, he was in all these films. After a while his agent would ring up the film companies and say, "Gielgud will do it but please could he have some direction." He couldn't think of going on the set and nobody giving him some direction. He was open, free and talented.' Even Sir John Gielgud, at ninety, knew that there was more for him to find as an actor and he knew that others could see it better. We'd all do well to take a similar attitude in life. An open mind, and an ability to take on board the views of experts in your field, is a powerful way to keep growing and developing your skills. It takes trust in yourself.

It's an incredibly useful life skill, to be able to take on someone else's view-point, without getting stressed out and defensive. In this section Alan Cumming's going to talk to you about dealing with your critics, analysing their motives and learning from them.

Alan Cumming

In all walks of life, people want you to fit into a mould and to be a type. If you want to be employed in a certain way there are certain skills you have to have and certain behaviours you have to acquire. Criticism can be useful for that.

When you're criticized, there's always an element of needing to lick your wounds and then start off again, put that behind you. It's also important to keep in perspective why it was said and what was the reason behind it. Sometimes people think you'll work better if you're criticized.

If it hurts, it's OK to think, wow I've been really side-swiped here and hurt, and not try just to think, 'Oh, I'm fine.' You're not fine when something like that happens. Be nice to yourself. Don't 'be brave'.

Then start to analyse it a bit. When I was younger it took me a long time to sort things out. You've got to sort through it. There may be other things going on. Often criticism says more about the person giving it to you. You can use it in a funny way as a spur. It can make you think, not necessarily that I'm going to show them, but I'm not going to let this drag me down. The only place you can go from there is up.

When you're clear-headed . . . move on. It's really important to think, I've had a bad day because somebody said this about me and tomorrow I'm moving forward. This is the worst I'm ever going to feel about it. It's going to get better from here on in. It's really important to be strong about how you feel. Other people won't have a positive experience or opinion about you that you don't have about yourself. But you are the most interesting thing about yourself. Your experience, what you've taken from life and how you look at life is what is most special about you.

The ability to take a note marks out the temperament of the good actor, and of the star in the real sense of the word. Specifically, a 'note' is the director's view of what you, the actor, can do to improve your performance. Even once the show is up and running a director will come in for 'notes'. They watch the show and when it's over, they tell you what you can do better.

The cardinal sin, and mark of an amateur, is to talk back. A professional actor is expected to want to receive criticism and to improve their performance. Very often if you hear nothing, it's because there's nothing to improve. You will never hear a professional actor make excuses. There are no excuses for being bad. If the director wants to tell you your performance was awful, you listen respectfully, and entertain the possibility that they are right. Then you have to work out how to make sense of it for yourself.

The business of 'notes' gives actors excellent skills in staying open to the views of someone else. It's an essential for star quality. I'm going to talk you through the most important rules to help you do the same in your life, whatever your profession.

First, choose who you listen to. Find your version of the director, and pay the most attention to them. You can even pay them! Sometimes a professional coach will give you the most honest feedback. They need to have a combination of expertise and your interests at heart. Most actors will tell you that they don't pay attention to the critics, whether it's positive or negative. Many take Samuel Goldwyn's advice about professional criticism: 'Don't pay any attention to the critics. Don't even ignore them.' Much better to take advice from those you trust.

Don't pay any attention to the critics. Don't even ignore them

Second, when you listen to criticism keep your behaviour separate from your identity. Someone may criticize you for being late. Keep reminding yourself that they are criticizing the lateness, the behaviour. You, as a person, have a separate and protected sense of inner worth. Acknowledge that you will work on your punctuality. It's only a behaviour.

Third, the really upsetting criticism is usually the kind that echoes the bad things we fear may be true in ourselves. When someone pinpoints one of your weak spots, that's when you implode. The secret is to learn to separate your inner, darkest vulnerabilities, from their point of view. Develop what Kathleen Turner calls her 'third eye'. It's a part of your consciousness that is able to rise above you, watching over you and guiding your choices. Kathleen gives the example of a car crash – the moment time slows to allow you to steer your way out of trouble. Have a sense of your awareness flying up above you to look down on the situation like a fly on the wall. Notice how you are able to distance yourself emotionally, and listen better. When you feel vulnerable to criticism apply your third eye. Observe the dynamic between you and the critic. Give yourself some perspective.

Fourth, how you absorb the criticism is important. Act as if they have your best interests at heart, and be grateful that someone is at least taking the time to give you some feedback. If it's critical, at least they're being honest. That's a gift in itself in a world where so many people won't tell you what they really think.

Fifth, do your own personal salvage operation when they're

not around. Analyse their motives, something that Laura Linney has described as 'excavating'. It helps to remember that criticism is as much about the person giving it as it is about you. It's never the 'truth', it's simply their perspective. Sometimes the hardest thing to hear is the most useful. And as Alan Cumming has told you, if you analyse it right you can use it as a spur.

In the end you simply have to trust your instinct. Minnie Driver believes it to be crucial: 'All of us have an innate sense of when somebody really has a point and when they don't. You have to go away and feel it through. You have to come to that decision yourself. I'm a huge gut feeler, I really feel that people don't trust their guts enough. Take the ego out of it and know that not 100 per cent of what everyone says is "right". They can just give you some pointers. You can always ask your friends, "Did I really do those things?" They can say, "You kind of did." Then it's putting into practice what they tell you. You try it, and it feels completely bogus and ridiculous, but a lot of it is trial and error. It's proper push-me-pull-you stuff, you have to stay open and protect yourself, not give yourself over entirely to the ministering.'

It's a fine balance, as Minnie says. If you want real star quality you'll make sure you master it. The greatest test of your equanimity is how you deal with rejection, criticism and vulnerability. Take the hit when it comes, keep things in perspective and move on as soon as you can. There's always another day.

Your toolkit

- **Accept what you're feeling**. The first step to dealing with a feeling is noticing it, and accepting it. So do it. Whatever you're feeling, go with it.
- **If you want to change your emotion – move.** If you don't like how you're feeling, do something physical, stand up, walk around. It shifts your state instantly.
- **Practise gratitude.** If you feel rejected or criticized, acknowledge it, but don't get locked into the dark tunnel of negativity. Remember there are some good things in your life too. Find a chink of gratitude to move you forward out of the darkness.
- **Criticism is a tool for growth.** Take what you need from it, analyse the motives of the person criticizing you, and use it as a spur. Separate your behaviour from your identity, and take the feedback as a tool to help you develop, rather than seeing it as an attack on who you are.

The Top 10
Star Qualities

I hope you've gleaned lots of practical tips and tricks from these experts in the field of world-class performance. Enjoy creating your own personal toolkit – I hope it brings you success and happiness.

Of course, you won't need to use these tools all the time. There are moments in your life when you are 'backstage'; when you're at home, or with your oldest friends you can relax, slump and be completely at ease. The star qualities are for your 'onstage' moments. They can be little life-savers if you have them to hand in difficult moments.

And here they are, the top ten:

1. Never let the opinions of others become your opinion of yourself.
2. Glamour is internal and the rest is window dressing.
3. You always have a choice about how you feel.
4. If you admire the way someone does something, you can learn to do it too.
5. When nerves hit, think 'how can I help?'

6. There's always more than one perspective – take time to listen fully and to understand others.
7. Great speeches are about clear thought, passion and compassion.
8. If you want to make your dream happen, make the vision clear and compelling.
9. When things go wrong, accept your emotion, be grateful for the things you've got, then move on.
10. Be yourself, everyone else is already taken.

For more information, contact me at www.carolinegoyder.co.uk

Try acting

Finally, acting is the reason I have the confidence to do my job, to speak to large audiences and quite possibly to write this book. If you'd like to learn more about the skills, you may want to consider the following:

- Join an amateur dramatics society. Try www.amdram.co.uk or www.amateurdramatics.com.
- Many drama schools run an Introduction to Acting course. Try www.cssd.ac.uk, or try one of the other major drama schools, which you can find at www.ncdt.co.uk, for their short courses.

This above all – to thine own self be true,
And it must follow, as the night the day,
Thou canst not then be false to any man.
Farewell – my blessing season this in thee!

Hamlet, Act 1, Scene 3

Source Notes

Material quoted from Sarah Jessica Parker, Kate Winslet, Gael Garcia Bernal, Ewan McGregor, Alan Cumming, Bill Nighy, Helen Mirren, Susan Sarandon, Frances McDormand, Sophie Myles, Damian Lewis, Anna Massey, Jenny Agutter, David Hare, Naomie Harris, Hayley Atwell, Minnie Driver, Emily Mortimer, David Thewlis, Eve Best, Gemma Jones, Sara Kestelman, Imelda Staunton, Mark Strong and Rufus Sewell comes from original interviews conducted by the author.

CHAPTER 1

page
6   Uta Hagen, *Respect for Acting*, Wiley, New York, 1973
8   Charlotte Chandler, *Bette Davis: The Girl Who Walked Home Alone*, Pocket Books, 2006
11   Pauline Clance and Suzanne Ines did the original

study, 'The impostor syndrome among high-achieving women', in 1978

13 O' Toole, Peter, *Loitering With Intent*. Macmillan, London, 1993

16 Oprah Winfrey interviews Salma Hayek in *O – The Oprah Magazine*, 2003

19 Uta Hagen, *Respect for Acting*, Wiley, New York, 1973

20 Viola Spolin and Paul Sills *Theatre Games For the Lone Actor*, Northwestern University Press, 2001

20 Sigourney Weaver interview with Chrissy Iley, *Daily Mail*, 2006

21 Dr Seuss mentioned by Angelina Jolie on *Inside The Actors Studio*

22 Oprah Winfrey interviews Salma Hayek in *O – The Oprah Magazine*, 2003

26 Will Smith, *Inside The Actors Studio*

27 Frank Bernieri quoted in *Psychologies*, Jan 2009

CHAPTER 2

page

32 Jamie Lee Curtis Blog, *Huffington Post*, February 2009

32 Salma Hayek in Rachel Zoe and Rose Apodaca, *Style A to Zoe: The Art of Fashion, Beauty, and Everything Glamour*, Grand Central Publishing, New York, 2008

33   Umberto Eco, interview, *FT Magazine*, 2007

35   Interview with Felicity Kendal, *Independent*, 2006

39   Michael Chekhov, *On the Technique of Acting*, Harper-Collins, London, 1991

42   Salma Hayek, interview with Oprah Winfrey

42   Whoopi Goldberg, interview with Jean Wyclef, Brant Publications, Inc., 1999

46   Salma Hayek in Rachel Zoe and Rose Apodaca, *Style A to Zoe*

CHAPTER 3

page

50   George Clooney quoted in Ian Parker's article 'Somebody has to be in control', *New Yorker*, 2008

52   Olsen Laney Marti, *The Introvert Advantage*, Workman, New York, 2002

53   Katharine Hepburn, *Me, Stories of My Life*, Penguin, London, 1991

53   Amy Adams quoted in the *Los Angeles Daily News*, 2007

54   Philip Seymour Hoffman television interview about *The Savages*, 2007

56   John Hurt interview, *Guardian*, May 2009

61   'Bacall still passes the acid test'; *Birmingham Post*, 2 February 2009

61   Luaine Lee, 'Glenn Close returning for second season of *Damages*', *Tribune-Review/Pittsburgh Tribune-Review*, Tribune-Review Publishing Company, 2008

64   Glenda Jackson, interviewed by voice coach Louise Kerr for MA Voice Studies Dissertation, Central School of Speech and Drama, London

65   Kathleen Turner, *Send Yourself Roses, and Other Ways to Take the Lead in life*, Headline, London, 2008

CHAPTER 4

page

78   Joan Allen interview with Gary Younge, *Guardian*, 23 July 2005

78   Uta Hagen, *Respect for Acting*, Wiley, New York, 1973

80   Cecil Beaton, 'The Secret of How to Startle', *Theatre Arts*, May 1957

86   Jane Fonda, *My Life So Far*, Random House, New York, 2005

90   Harriet Walter, *Other People's Shoes*, Nick Hern Books, London, 2005

92   Fiona Shaw quoted in *Performing Women: Stand-ups, Strumpets and Itinerants*, Palgrave Macmillan, London, 2005

CHAPTER 5

CHAPTER 6

151   Oprah Winfrey interviews Salma Hayek in *O – The Oprah Magazine*, 2003

151   Michael Grinder, *Charisma – The Art of Relationships*

153   Thomas Harris, *I'm OK You're OK*, Arrow, London, 1995

156   This exercise is closely based on Robert Dilts' metaposition exercise. www.nlpu.com, or www.ppdlearning.co.uk

158   Rupert Everett, *Red Carpets and Banana Skins*, Abacus, London, 2006

CHAPTER 7

page

160   Laura Linney quoted in 'Women in Hollywood' article on premiere.com, 2005

163   Forest Whitaker, *Inside the Actors' Studio*

168   Dr Eric Berne MD, *What Do You Say After You Say Hello?*, Corgi, 1974

170   Noel Coward with Sheridan Morley, *Present Indicative: The First Autobiography of Noel Coward*, Methuen, London, 2004

182   Laura Linney quoted in 'Women in Hollywood' article on premiere.com, 2005

186   Simon Callow, *Being an Actor*, Vintage, Random House, London, 2004

187   Ewan McGregor interview, *The Speaker*, BBC

CHAPTER 8

page

194 Will Smith, *Inside the Actors' Studio*

197 Michele Norris, 'Peter O'Toole and a Young "Venus"', *NPR All Things Considered*, 2007

197 Will Smith, Speech at Prince's Trust Event

197 Katharine Hepburn, *Me*, Penguin, London, 1992

198 Oprah Winfrey interviews Salma Hayek in *O – The Oprah Magazine*, 2003

204 Csikszentmihali Mihaly, *Flow – The Classic Work On How to Achieve Happiness*, Rider, 1992

200 Tony Curtis, *American Prince: My Autobiography*, Virgin, London, 2008

204 Konstantin Stanislavsky, *Creating a Role*, Methuen Drama, London, 1981

206 Morgan Freeman, *Inside the Actors' Studio*

214 Max Atkinson's book, *Lend Me Your Ears* (Random House, 2004) is great on the power of pauses

216 Michael Caine interview, *Sunday Telegraph*, April 2009

216 Ethan Hawke, *Inside the Actors' Studio*

216 Csikszentmihali Mihaly, *Flow*

219 Morgan Freeman, *Inside the Actors' Studio*

220 Amy Adams quoted in the Los Angeles *Daily News*, 2007

220   Tom Hanks, *Inside the Actors' Studio*

222   This strategy was modelled by Robert Dilts, who looked at other strategies of genius. His writing and his work in NLP is well worth exploring: www.nlpu.com in the US or www.ppdlearning.co.uk in the UK

CHAPTER 9

page

226   Luaine Lee, 'Glenn Close returning for second season of *Damages*', *Tribune-Review/Pittsburgh Tribune-Review*

226   Oprah Winfrey interviews Salma Hayek in *O – The Oprah Magazine*, 2003

234   Viola Spolin, *Theater Games for the Lone Actor*, North-Western University Press, 2001

235   Will Smith, *Inside The Actors Studio*

240   Viola Spolin, *Theater Games for the Lone Actor*

241   Johnny Depp, *Inside the Actors' Studio*

241   Martin E. P. Seligman, *Authentic Happiness, Using The New Positive Psychology To Realize Your Potential For Lasting Fulfilment*, Nicholas Brealey Publishing, 2003

241   R. Emmons and M. McCullough, *The Grateful Disposition: A Conceptual and Empirical Topography: Journal of*

Personality and Social Psychology, 2002, 82, 112–127

241   Robert A. Emmons, *Thanks! How the New Science of Gratitude Can Make you Happier*, Houghton Mifflin, New York, 2007

242   Samuel Beckett, *Worstword Ho*, Calder Publications, London, 1984

243   Peter Barkworth, *About Acting*, Methuen, London, 1980

243   Luaine Lee, 'Glenn Close returning for second season of *Damages*', *Tribune-Review/Pittsburgh Tribune-Review*

248   Kathleen Turner, *Send Yourself Roses, and Other Ways to Take the Lead in life*, Headline, London, 2008

Acknowledgements

Heartfelt thanks go to all the actors and their agents, friends and assistants who helped with the book. You made it possible and I am eternally grateful; Jenny Agutter, Eileen Atkins, Hayley Atwell, Gael Garcia Bernal, Eve Best, Alan Cumming, Minnie Driver, David Hare, Naomie Harris, Gemma Jones, Sara Kestelman, Damian Lewis, Anna Massey, Frances McDormand, Ewan McGregor, Helen Mirren, Emily Mortimer, Sophia Myles, Bill Nighy, Sarah Jessica Parker, Susan Sarandon, Rufus Sewell, Imelda Staunton, Mark Strong, David Thewlis and Kate Winslet. Particular thanks also to Sandy Campbell, Daisy Lewis, Sarah Wolf, Sara Keene, Jemma Kearney and Melinda Relyea.

To Amy Gadney (you started it and nurtured it in the poshest greasy spoon in town), Sara Kestelman and Fiamma Montagu – you all inspired and helped in so many ways and in so many different stages. Goddesses all.

There are three crucial people to the existence of this book, without whom it would have remained a lovely idea. To all three I am completely, eternally indebted.

Fiona Harrold – You are a fairy godmother. Once upon a time you spurred me to action, told me the challenge was to think big enough (the best advice ever) and then kept me on track when I got vertigo. You are a genius first reader, and simply, I couldn't have done it without you.

Jonny Geller – Your email is carved into my consciousness, because it's when it started. You instantly understood what it was all about and believed in it, and inspired me, making it possible, real and exciting. You were tough when it mattered. Then you worked magic. I owe you heartfelt thanks. Many, many thanks also to Melissa Pimentel for all your support on the long journey to the book.

Ingrid Connell – Thank you for loving the book the way I do! When you said yes, it was one of the best (and scariest) days of my life. You've been such a fantastically kind and thoughtful editor and have steered the book intuitively and gently to its gorgeous final form. Big thanks also to Tania Adams, Helen Guthrie, Kate Hewson, Iram Allam, Kath Walker, and the team at Macmillan who have brought the book to life.

Thanks to all at Central School of Speech and Drama (past and present). To my students who teach me at least as much as I teach them! To Bruce Wooding, David Carey, Barbara

Houseman, Caitlin Adams, Andy Lavender, Annie Morrison, Debbie Green, Wendy Gadian, David Willis, Ben Buratta, Gregory Duke, Anne Walsh, Emily Pollet, Debbie Scully, Geoff Colman, Helen Lederer and Heather Francis for helping in different ways during (and before) the project.

Big thanks also to Katie Bond, Randall Reale, Michel, Henryk Hetflaisz, Jasia Ward, Jana Sanchez, Sarah Baynes, Tim Bevan, Tamara Hill-Norton and Dan Hind for amazing help at different stages. To Tal-y-Bont and Gainford for peace and quiet and birdsong.

Thank you to the girls – you have been a real support during the writing of this book; Annika Bosanquet, Carissa Bub, Charlotte Stone, Christina Blake, Nathalie Bristow, Nicola Franks, Nicky Mudie and Louise Dumayne. I'm sorry I've been such a hermit! To my lovely boys – Jacques and Jimmy. Here's hoping you are up for trips to the theatre in a few years.

To my parents who've been there unconditionally – even for a drama queen! To my brother Joe who came up with a brilliant title and to Fiona, Tabitha and Barney. To Dorothy. To my grandmother Rosemary, who epitomizes the light inside.

Finally to Tom – who said he didn't want to be acknowledged, but you should know how stubborn I am! Your support has made it possible, and you're a star.

Index

in interviews 118–25, 26
relaxing others 72–3
speeches and presentations
180–1, 192
see also mind and body; nerves,
controlling
resilience 216–22, 223, 236–43
responsibility in conflicts 136–39
rhythm, of character 92
Ribot, Theodule Amand 59
Richardson, Sir Ralph 228
risk taking 27, 163–70
Roddick, Anita 80
Rodenburg, Patsy 47
Romany gypsies 241
Royal Academy of Dramatic Art
(RADA) 13–14, 38
Ruskin, John 123

Sarandon, Susan 6, 21, 22
Sartre, Jean-Paul 136
Scott Fitzgerald, F 131
self-consciousness, overcoming
144
inhibitions 95–100
at parties 70
with physicality 39–40, 41
see also confidence
self-image 80, 83–5, 101
self-knowledge 13–14, 139
see also rejection and critiscism
self-respect 151, 153–5
see also confidence

Seligman, Professor Martin 110
'sense memory' 60
sensuality, using 40–1, 46, 47–8
Seuss, Dr Theodor 21
Sewell, Rufus 14–15, 124, 239–40
Shakespeare, William 3, 86, 99
Shaw, Fiona 92
shyness 51–2, 73, 83–4, 91
see also confidence; self-consciousness
Smith, Dame Maggie 35
Smith, Paul 80
Smith, Will 26, 194, 197, 235
Snow, Jon 80
Snyder, Professor C R 110
Spacey, Kevin 207, 230
speeches *see* presentations and
speeches
Spolin, Viola 20, 234, 240,
242–3
'spotlight effect' 70
Stanislavsky, Konstantin 24, 73,
90, 211
emotion memory 58, 59
moment of orientation 64
'communion' 71, 72
pursuit of goals 201, 212
'self-forgetful' 40
status 140–1
adapting your 142–50
body language 148–9, 157–8
voice 147–8, 149, 157
see also image